THE BLUE ROAD TO TRUMP HELL

How Corporate Democrats Paved the Way for Autocracy

Norman Solomon

With Cartoons by **Matt Wuerker**

The Blue Road to Trump Hell was co-published in December 2025 by ColdType and Progressive Hub in original paperback and digital formats.

The website for this book is:
blueroad.info

ISBN 979-8-9936900-0-1 (paperback)
ISBN 979-8-9936900-1-8 (e-book)
ISBN 979-8-9936900-2-5 (PDF)

Five pieces in this book were co-written with Jeff Cohen and published on May 9, 2021; Nov. 10, 2021; Nov. 26, 2023; Jan. 11, 2024; July 5, 2024.

To learn more about Norman Solomon, visit:
normansolomon.com

To learn more about Matt Wuerker, visit:
politico.com/staff/matt-wuerker

To learn more about ColdType, visit:
coldtype.net

To learn more about Progressive Hub, visit:
progressivehub.net

Designed and produced by
ColdType editor, Tony Sutton.

RIGHT
LEFT
M.WUERKER

Norman Solomon is the national director of RootsAction and executive director of the Institute for Public Accuracy. He is the author of more than a dozen books including *War Made Invisible: How America Hides the Human Toll of Its Military Machine.* Solomon has written about politics for many publications including *The Hill, The Nation,* the *Guardian, Common Dreams,* the *Los Angeles Times* and *Salon.*

Matt Wuerker has been *Politico*'s editorial cartoonist and illustrator since its 2007 launch. In 2012, he won the Pulitzer Prize for editorial cartooning. During the past several decades, his work has appeared in publications ranging from the *Washington Post* and the *New York Times* to *Smithsonian* and *The Nation,* among many others.

But the stars that marked our starting fall away.
We must go deeper into greater pain,
for it is not permitted that we stay.
– *Dante's Inferno*

In a murderous time
   the heart breaks and breaks
      and lives by breaking.
It is necessary to go
   through dark and deeper dark
      And not to turn.
– *Stanley Kunitz*

Pessimism of the intellect,
optimism of the will.
– *Romain Rolland*

The only hope is
in the struggle.
– *India Walton*

Contents

Introduction

THE DEMOCRATIC PARTY ENABLED DONALD TRUMP TO BECOME president twice because of repetition compulsions that still plague the top echelons of the party – undermining its potential to end the real-life nightmare of MAGA control over the federal government.

This book scrutinizes how the behavior of many Democrats assisted Trump's electoral triumphs. That scrutiny is important not only for clarity about the past. It also makes possible a focus on ways that such failures can be avoided in the future.

The Blue Road to Trump Hell is lined with warning signs that Democratic Party leaders and mass media routinely denied or ignored. I wrote the chapters from 2016 to 2024 in real time. Nothing has been revised for hindsight.

The last chapter, "2025 and Beyond," assesses how top Democrats responded to the escalating repression from the Trump regime after his return to the White House.

2016

Barack Obama's last year as president was supposed to lead to Hillary Clinton's first. But by 2016 the people who had twice elected Obama were not nearly as content as most Democratic Party leaders wanted to believe.

Elites did well after Obama took office in January 2009 amid the Great Recession. He continued with predecessor George W. Bush's "practice of bailing out the bankers while ignoring the anguish their toxic mortgage packages caused the rest of us," journalist Robert Scheer pointed out. By the time Obama was most of the way through his presidency, journalist David Dayen wrote, he had enabled "the dispossession of at least 5.2 million U.S. homeowner families, the explosion of inequality, and the largest ruination of middle-class wealth in nearly a century."

Hillary Clinton offered more of the status quo. Her allies in the Democratic Party and in corporate media pulled out all the stops so she could win the party's presidential nomination. She was able to prevail over the strong primary challenge from progressive populist Bernie Sanders. Her campaign trail went downhill from there.

Hillary
IT'S THE ECONOMY, STUPID!
Bernie
Hillary
Bernie
WELL, ISN'T THAT IRONIC?!
M.WUERKER
POLITICO Universal Uclick

Spin Shift on Bernie: The Escalating Media Assault

January 27, 2016

FOR A LONG TIME, AS HE CAMPAIGNED FOR PRESIDENT, A WIDE spectrum of establishment media insisted that Bernie Sanders couldn't win. Now they're sounding the alarm that he might.

And, just in case you haven't gotten the media message yet – Sanders is "angry," kind of like Donald Trump.

Elite media often blur distinctions between right-wing populism and progressive populism – as though there's not all that much difference between appealing to xenophobia and racism on the one hand and appealing for social justice and humanistic solidarity on the other.

Many journalists can't resist lumping Trump and Sanders together as rabble-rousing outliers. But in the real world, the differences are vast.

Donald Trump is to Bernie Sanders as Archie Bunker is to Jon Stewart.

Among regular *New York Times* columnists, aversion to Bernie Sanders has become more pronounced in recent days at both ends of the newspaper's ideological spectrum, such as it is. Republican Party aficionado David Brooks (whose idea of a good political time is Marco Rubio) has been freaking out in print, most recently with a Tuesday column headlined "Stay Sane America, Please!"

Brooks warned that his current nightmare for the nation is in triplicate – President Trump, President Cruz or President Sanders. For Brooks, all three contenders appear to be about equally awful; Trump is "one of the most loathed men in American public life," while "America has never elected a candidate maximally extreme from the political center, the way Sanders and Cruz are."

That "political center" of power sustains huge income inequality, perpetual war, scant action on climate change and reflexive support for the latest unhinged escalation of the nuclear arms race. In other words, what C. Wright Mills called "crackpot realism."

Meanwhile, liberal *Times* columnist Paul Krugman (whose idea of a good political time is Hillary Clinton) keeps propounding a stand-on-head formula for social change – a kind of trickle-down theory of political power, in which "happy dreams" must yield to "hard thinking," a euphemism for crackpot realism.

An excellent rejoinder has come from former Labor Secretary Robert Reich. "Krugman doesn't get it," Reich wrote. "I've been in and around Washington for almost 50 years, including a stint in the cabinet, and I've learned that real change happens only when a substantial share of the American public is mobilized, organized, energized, and determined to make it happen."

And Reich added: "Political 'pragmatism' may require accepting 'half loaves' – but the full loaf has to be large and bold enough in the first place to make the half loaf meaningful. That's why the movement must aim high – toward a single-payer universal health, free public higher education, and busting up the biggest banks, for example."

But for mainline media, exploring such substance is low priority, much lower than facile labeling and horseracing… and riffing on how Bernie Sanders sounds "angry."

On "Morning Edition," this week began with NPR political reporter Mara Liasson telling listeners that "Bernie Sanders' angry tirades against Wall Street have found a receptive audience." (Meanwhile, without anger or tirades, "Hillary Clinton often talks about the fears and insecurities of ordinary voters.")

The momentum of the Sanders campaign will soon provoke a lot more corporate media attacks along the lines of a *Chicago Tribune* editorial that appeared in print on Monday. The newspaper editorialized that nomination of Trump, Cruz or Sanders "could be politically disastrous," and it declared: "Wise heads in both parties are verging on panic."

Such panic has just begun, among party elites and media elites. Eager to undermine Sanders, the *Tribune* editorial warned that as a "self-declared democratic socialist," Sanders "brandishes a label that, a Gallup poll found, would automatically make him unacceptable to nearly half the public."

A strong critique of such commentaries has come from the media watch group FAIR, where Jim Naureckas pointed out that "voters would not be asked to vote for 'a socialist' – they'd be asked to vote for Bernie Sanders. And while pollsters don't include Sanders in general election matchups as often as they do Hillary Clinton, they have asked how the Vermont senator would do against various Republicans – and he generally does pretty well. In particular, against the candidate the *Tribune* says is 'best positioned' to 'capture the broad, sensible center' – Jeb Bush – Sanders leads in polls by an average of 3.0 percentage points, based on polling analysis by the website *Real Clear Politics.*"

In mass media, the conventional sensibilities of pundits like Brooks and Krugman, reporters like Liasson, and outlets like the *Chicago Tribune* routinely get the first and last words. Here, the last ones are from Naureckas:

> When pollsters match Sanders against the four top-polling Republican hopefuls, on average he does better than Clinton does against each of them – even though she, like Bush, is supposed to be "best positioned" to "capture the broad, sensible center," according to the *Tribune*.
>
> Actually, the elements of Sanders' platform that elite media are most likely to associate with "socialism" – things like universal, publicly funded healthcare and eliminating tuition at public colleges – are quite popular with the public, and go a long way to explain his favorable poll numbers. But they are also the sort of proposals that make Sanders unacceptable to the nation's wealthy elite – and to establishment media outlets.

The Bernie Campaign: The Democratic Party's Biggest Insurrection in Decades

February 1, 2016

FORTY-EIGHT YEARS AGO, A SERIOUS INSURRECTION JEOPARD-ized the power structure of the national Democratic Party for the first time in memory. Propelled by the movement against the Vietnam War, that grassroots uprising cast a big electoral shadow soon after Senator Eugene McCarthy dared to challenge the incumbent for the Democratic presidential nomination.

When 1968 got underway, the news media were scoffing at McCarthy's antiwar campaign as quixotic and doomed. But in the nation's leadoff New Hampshire primary, McCarthy received 42 percent of the vote while President Lyndon B. Johnson couldn't quite get to 50 percent – results that were shattering for LBJ. Suddenly emboldened, Senator Robert Kennedy quickly entered the race. Two weeks later, Johnson announced that he wouldn't seek re-election.

Although the nomination eventually went to Johnson's vice president Hubert Humphrey – a supporter of the war who was the choice of Democratic power brokers – the unmasking of the party's undemocratic process led to internal reforms that aided the Democratic Party's second modern insurrection. It came four years later, when Senator George McGovern won the presidential nomination, thanks to grassroots movements involving young people and activists of color. But any sense of triumph disappeared in the wake of President Nixon's landslide re-election in November 1972.

The third major insurrection came in 1988, when Jesse Jackson led a dynamic, multiracial "rainbow" campaign for president that had major impacts on the national stage. (His previous campaign, in '84, had been relatively weak.) The 1988 primaries and caucuses were hard-fought, state by state, with rainbow activists working shoulder-to-shoulder, whether focused on issues of class, race or gender. (Back then, Jackson was a gutsy voice for social justice, for human rights and against war – much more willing to confront the Democratic Party establishment than he is now.) At the contentious Democratic National Convention that summer in Atlanta, where Jackson delegates were highly visible as 30 percent of the total, the old guard closed ranks behind nominee Michael Dukakis.

Now, as February 2016 gets underway, we're in the midst of the first major insurrection against the Democratic Party power structure in 28 years. The millions of us who support the Bernie Sanders campaign – whatever our important criticisms – should aim to fully grasp the huge opportunities and obstacles that await us.

Of the three previous insurrections, only one gained the nomination, and none won the presidency. Corporate capitalism – wielding its muscular appendage, mass media – can be depended upon to take off the gloves and pummel the insurrection's candidate to the extent that the campaign has gained momentum. That happened to McCarthy, McGovern and Jackson. It's now happening to Sanders.

The last days of January brought one big-daily newspaper editorial after another after another attacking Bernie with vehemence and vitriol. The less unlikely his winning of the nomination gets, the more that mega-media assaults promoting absurdities will intensify.

Meanwhile – at least as long as her nomination is threatened from the left – Hillary Clinton will benefit from corporate biases that wallpaper the mass-media echo chambers. The Sunday *New York Times* editorial endorsing Clinton could hardly be more fanciful and hagiographic if written by her campaign.

Many of the same media outlets and overall corporate forces that denounced Eugene McCarthy in 1968, George McGovern in 1972 and Jesse Jackson in 1988 are gunning for Bernie Sanders in 2016. We shouldn't be surprised. But we should be ready, willing and able to do our own messaging – widely and intensely – in communities across the country.

At the same time, we should not confuse electoral campaigns with long-term political organizing. Campaigns for office are quite different matters than the more transformative task of building progressive infrastructure – and vibrant coalitions – that can endure and grow, year after year.

Genuinely progressive candidates can inspire and galvanize – and sometimes they can even win. But election campaigns, especially national ones, are almost always boom/bust. Sometimes they can help to fuel movement momentum, but they aren't the engine.

Election campaigns are distinct from movements even if they converge for a while, no matter what pundits and campaign spinners say. Candidates often want to harness social movements for their campaigns. But our best approach is to view electoral campaigns as – at best – subsets of movements, not the other way around.

The Bernie campaign could be a watershed for progressive organizing through the rest of this decade and beyond. That will largely depend on what activists do – in the next weeks, months and years.

Hillary Clinton's Millennial Problem Runs Deep

October 7, 2016

IF THIS COUNTRY HAD A MAXIMUM VOTING AGE OF 35, HILLARY Clinton would now be in danger of losing the election to Libertarian Party candidate Gary Johnson.

Last month, support for the Democratic nominee among millennials who are likely voters fell to within 2 percent of their support for Johnson, according to a Quinnipiac poll. If you add in the substantial millennial support for Green Party candidate Jill Stein, the pair of third-party nominees outpolled Clinton 44 percent to 31 percent.

How can this be?

After seeing under-35 voters go overwhelmingly for Bernie Sanders during the primary season, Clinton has continued to lose ground with them. The core problem is that Clinton was being candid 13 months ago when she told a Women for Hillary audience in Ohio: "You know, I get accused of being kind of moderate and center. I plead guilty."

Most millennials don't want a president who is "kind of moderate and center" – nor are they drawn to belated progressive rhetoric without a record to back it up.

The Sanders campaign gained enthusiastic support because the candidate's consistent record of progressive substance matched his oratory. Clinton strains to seem like an authentic progressive because she isn't.

In recent months, the former secretary of state has made mostly formulaic efforts to reach out to the left-leaning young, many of whom are inclined to vote third-party or not vote at all in November. Relying on conventional party wisdom, she hasn't seemed to grasp the power of idealism among young voters – who are now having a hard time shifting from feeling the Bern to holding their nose, which is what it would take for a lot of them to vote for Clinton.

Today the independent Bernie Delegates Network is releasing the results of a survey that we conducted in recent days among Sanders delegates to the Democratic National Convention. Four hundred and sixty-one of those delegates participated in the straw poll. Results from the survey reflect the reality that Clinton has not made the sale to many of the often-young supporters of Sanders's presidential campaign:

- 37 percent of Sanders delegates said they plan to vote for Clinton. (Those delegates were not more inclined to vote for her if they live in a swing state where the race is close.)

- 33 percent said they plan to vote for Stein.

- 17 percent said they were undecided on how to cast their presidential ballot.

Among the polled Sanders delegates, less than 1 percent said they would vote for Johnson, and the same was true for GOP nominee Donald Trump.

Thanks to Trump's erratic and dangerous candidacy, Clinton will probably win the election – but her chances would be better if she could build bridges with the vast majority of millennials who don't like Trump.

For her prospective presidency, Clinton has made only one irrevocable big decision this year: selecting Tim Kaine for the VP slot. While hailed by Washington's punditocracy, the choice was a dismissive message to Bernie's base.

A strong defender of Virginia's anti-union "right to work" law as governor, Kaine went on to take positions in the Senate that are anathema to progressives. In 2011 he criticized fellow Democrats for advocating a higher tax rate for millionaires. Last year, Kaine was one of just a dozen Democratic senators to vote for fast-tracking the controversial Trans-Pacific Partnership trade deal. (In early summer, a straw poll of Sanders delegates found that stopping the TPP was their top priority.)

Selection of Kaine was just the start of assembling a decidedly pro-corporate and anti-progressive squad for the future. The Clinton transition team, chaired by corporate champion Ken Salazar, has been stocked with strong advocates for the TPP and numerous other major policy positions favored by Wall Street.

Clinton's long career of sounding progressive yet proceeding otherwise hardly inspires confidence in her recent embraces of forward-looking proposals, such as free tuition at public colleges for families with annual incomes of $125,000 or less.

In short, after rallying behind Bernie Sanders's genuine economic populism, many young people don't trust the pseudo-populism of Hillary Clinton's campaign. She has earned a millennial problem that could prevent her from becoming president.

For the Trump Era:
Fight Not Flight

November 10, 2016

A LOT OF U.S. CITIZENS ARE NOW TALKING ABOUT LEAVING THE country. Canada, Europe and New Zealand are popular scenarios. Moving abroad might be an individual solution. But the social solution is to stay and put up a fight.

The most right-wing U.S. government in our lifetimes will soon have its executive and legislative branches under reactionary control, with major ripple effects on the judiciary. All the fixings for a dystopian future will be on the table.

In a realistic light, the outlook is awfully grim. No wonder a huge number of people in the United States are struggling with mixtures of grief, anger, frustration, fear.

If Donald Trump and major forces backing him get their way, the conditions described by Frederick Douglass – still all too prevalent now – will worsen in the years ahead: "Where justice is denied, where poverty is enforced, where ignorance prevails, and where any one class is made to feel that society is an organized conspiracy to oppress, rob, and degrade them, neither persons nor property will be safe."

As James Baldwin wrote, "People who shut their eyes to reality simply invite their own destruction, and anyone who insists on remaining in a state of innocence long after that innocence is dead turns himself into a monster."

Those quotes from Douglass and Baldwin are in a book of paintings by Robert Shetterly, *Americans Who Tell the Truth*. Another portrait in the collection appears under these words from Helen Keller: "When one comes to think of it, there are no such things as divine, immutable, or inalienable rights. Rights are things we get when we are strong enough to make good our claim on them."

That statement from Keller aptly describes our current predicament and possibilities. The impending Trump presidency is a direct threat to basic human rights. To make good our claim on those rights will require that we become "strong enough," individually and collectively.

Gaining such strength will require that we provide much more support for independent progressive institutions – the array of organizations that can serve as collective bulwarks against the momentum of systemic greed, bigotry, massive violence, economic exploitation and environmental destruction.

We're now being flung into a new era that will intensify many of the oppressive aspects of the U.S. governmental apparatus and political economy. An ongoing imperative will be to mitigate serious-to-catastrophic damage in many realms. We need a united front – against the very real threat of severe repression that could morph into some form of fascism.

At this highly precarious time, progressives certainly don't need the tempests of factional disputes and ideological battles. And we certainly don't need the kind of reflexive capitulation that so often comes from the upper reaches of the Democratic Party. We're at the start of a protracted crisis that could become cataclysmic. We need progressive unity and unrelenting determination.

Only with eyes wide open do we have a real chance to understand clearly and organize effectively against the Trump regime. Failure to put up a fight should be unthinkable.

2017

From the outset, the words "President Trump" and the realities of his power were shocks to the system. Yet the system largely accommodated the new Trump administration as it swiftly broke all previous records for shameless and flagrant lying. Along the way, the sharp swerve rightward moved to normalize misogyny, racism, xenophobia and other assorted bigotries.

Meanwhile, Democratic Party leaders could hardly blame themselves or their presidential nominee Hillary Clinton for the virtually unbelievable circumstance of the Trump presidency. A critical focus on her coziness with Wall Street wouldn't do. Neither would critiquing her thinly veiled contempt for the progressive wing of the party. But faulting Russia became a persistent theme.

Flailing around for a consistent message while both the House and Senate were under Republican control, most Democrats did little more than point to some of Trump's dangerous actions or mere devious idiocies, without offering strong alternative programs. At the same time, Trump and his dutiful congressional allies set about dismantling just about any aspect of decent governance that they could.

FOX
TRUMP
Goldman Sachs
GET YOUR
SWAG HERE!
TRUMP™
UNOFFICIAL
SOUVENIR
GUIDE TO
THE
DONALD J.
TRUMP
INAUGURAL
PARADE
ALT-RIGHT COUNTRY
MARCHING BAND
FBI
PRESIDENT
UNITED STATES
M.WUERKER
POLITICO   Andrews McMeel Syn

The Democratic Party's Anti-Bernie Elites Have a Huge Stake in Blaming Russia

April 20, 2017

AFTER HILLARY CLINTON'S DEVASTATING LOSS NEARLY SIX months ago, her most powerful Democratic allies feared losing control of the party. Efforts to lip-synch economic populism while remaining closely tied to Wall Street had led to a catastrophic defeat. In the aftermath, the party's progressive base – personified by Bernie Sanders – was in position to start flipping over the corporate game board.

Aligned with Clinton, the elites of the Democratic Party needed to change the subject. Clear assessments of the national ticket's failures were hazardous to the status quo within the party. So were the groundswells of opposition to unfair economic privilege. So were the grassroots pressures for the party to become a genuine force for challenging big banks, Wall Street and overall corporate power.

In short, the Democratic Party's anti-Bernie establishment needed to reframe the discourse in a hurry. And – in tandem with mass media – it did.

The reframing could be summed up in two words: Blame Russia.

By early winter, the public discourse was going sideways – much to the benefit of party elites. The meme of blaming Russia and Vladimir Putin for the election of Donald Trump effectively functioned to let the Wall Street-friendly leadership of the national Democratic Party off the hook. Meanwhile, serious attempts to focus on the ways that wounds to democracy in the United States have been self-inflicted – whether via the campaign finance system or the purging of minorities from voter rolls or any number of other systemic injustices – were largely set aside.

Fading from scrutiny was the establishment that continued to dominate the Democratic Party's superstructure. At the same time, its devotion to economic elites was undiminished. As Bernie told a reporter on the last day of February: "Certainly there are some people in the

Democratic Party who want to maintain the status quo. They would rather go down with the Titanic so long as they have first-class seats."

Amid great luxury and looming catastrophe, the party's current hierarchy has invested enormous political capital in depicting Vladimir Putin as an unmitigated arch villain. Relevant history was irrelevant, to be ignored or denied.

With dutiful conformity from most Democrats in Congress, the party elites doubled, tripled and quadrupled down on the emphatic claim that Moscow is the capital of, by any other name, an evil empire. Rather than just calling for what's needed – a truly independent investigation into allegations that the Russian government interfered with the U.S. election – the party line became hyperbolic and unmoored from the available evidence.

Given their vehement political investment in demonizing Russia's President Putin, Democratic leaders are oriented to seeing the potential of detente with Russia as counterproductive in terms of their electoral strategy for 2018 and 2020. It's a calculus that boosts the risks of nuclear annihilation, given the very real dangers of escalating tensions between Washington and Moscow.

Along the way, top party officials seem bent on returning to a kind of pre-Bernie-campaign doldrums. The new chair of the Democratic National Committee, Tom Perez, can't bring himself to say that the power of Wall Street is antithetical to the interests of working people. That reality came to painful light this week during a live appearance on national television.

During a 10-minute joint interview along with Bernie Sanders on Tuesday night, Perez was a font of exactly the kind of trite empty slogans and worn-out platitudes that oiled the engines of the dismal Clinton campaign.

While Sanders was forthright, Perez was evasive. While Sanders talked about systemic injustice, Perez fixated on Trump. While Sanders pointed to a way forward for realistic and far-reaching progressive change, Perez hung onto a rhetorical formula that expressed support for victims of the economic order without acknowledging the existence of victimizers.

In an incisive article published by *The Nation* magazine, Robert

Borosage wrote last week: "For all the urgent pleas for unity in the face of Trump, the party establishment has always made it clear that they mean unity under their banner. That's why they mobilized to keep the leader of the Congressional Progressive Caucus, Representative Keith Ellison, from becoming head of the DNC. It's why the knives are still out for Sanders and those who supported him."

While Bernie is hardly a reliable opponent of U.S. war policies, he is significantly more critical of U.S. military intervention than the Democratic Party leaders who often champion it. Borosage noted that the party establishment is locked into militaristic orthodoxies that favor continuing to inflict the kind of disasters that the United States has brought to Iraq, Libya and other countries: "Democrats are in the midst of a major struggle to decide what they stand for and who they represent. Part of that is the debate over a bipartisan interventionist foreign policy that has so abjectly failed."

For the Democratic Party's most hawkish wing – dominant from the top down and allied with Clinton's de facto neocon approach to foreign policy – the U.S. government's April 6 cruise missile attack on a Syrian airfield was an indication of real leverage for more war. That attack on a close ally of Russia showed that incessant Russia-baiting of Trump can get gratifying military results for the Democratic elites who are undaunted in their advocacy of regime change in Syria and elsewhere.

The politically motivated missile attack on Syria showed just how dangerous it is to keep Russia-baiting Trump, giving him political incentive to prove how tough he is on Russia after all. What's at stake includes the imperative of preventing a military clash between the world's two nuclear superpowers. But the corporate hawks at the top of the national Democratic Party have other priorities.

Behind the Media Surge Against Bernie Sanders

June 18, 2017

IT'S ROUTINE FOR RIGHT-WING OUTLETS LIKE FOX TO SMEAR progressive activists under the guise of "news" coverage. But why the *New York Times*? And why the special venom for Bernie Sanders?

After the horrific June 14 shooting of Congressman Steve Scalise and three other participants in a Republican baseball practice, the media floodgates opened for slimy innuendos. Before the day was done, a major supplier of the political sewage was the *New York Times*, which prominently published a left-blaming article that masqueraded as news reporting.

The media watch group FAIR pointed out that the *Times* piece "started with a false premise and patched together a dodgy piece of innuendo and guilt-by-association in order to place the blame for a shooting in Virginia on 'the most ardent supporters of Senator Bernie Sanders.'"

It would be a mistake to think that the *Times* story was only the result of bias inflamed by the grisly shooting spree. A few days earlier, the newspaper had front-paged another "news" story hostile to grass-roots political forces aligned with Bernie – a de facto editorial masquerading as news coverage, headlined: "Democrats in Split-Screen: The Base Wants It All. The Party Wants to Win."

In a bizarre disconnect from electoral reality, the article portrayed a party establishment that had lost election after election, including a cataclysmic loss to Trump, as being about winning. And the article portrayed the party's activist base as interfering with the establishment's winning ways.

Such *Times* stories are now operating under a heightened sense of journalistic impunity since the newspaper abolished its 14-year-old ombudsperson position of "public editor" more than two weeks ago – further insulating its reporters and editors from accountability. More than ever, calling the shots at the *Times* – the most influential news outlet in the United States – means never having to say you're sorry, or even justify what you've done.

Corporate-owned media hostility toward Sanders and the progressive base has been conspicuous and well-documented. That hostility started early in his campaign and never let up, sometimes manifested as giving him scant coverage. When the momentum of the Bernie campaign gained powerful traction as a threat to the corporate order, big media efforts to trash him went over the top.

At a key political moment last year, as FAIR analyst Adam Johnson wrote, "the *Washington Post* ran 16 negative stories on Bernie Sanders in 16 hours, between roughly 10:20 PM EST Sunday, March 6, to 3:54 PM EST Monday, March 7 – a window that includes the crucial Democratic debate in Flint, Michigan, and the next morning's spin." The day after this onslaught, Sanders stunned the elite pundit class by winning the Michigan primary.

Now, in mid-2017, with no presidential election in sight, why is the corporate media hostility toward Sanders so prone to surface?

Consider, as an example, this structural reality: Jeff Bezos, the owner of the *Washington Post*, has just unveiled plans for his company Amazon to buy Whole Foods. And Bernie Sanders, the most popular politician in the United States according to polls, is strongly opposed to allowing such huge consolidations of corporate power.

For good reasons, media powerhouses like the *New York Times* and *Washington Post* are averse to Donald Trump. At the same time, they remain quite cozy with Hillary Clinton's political orientation and especially with the sectors of the corporate-military establishment that she represents. Like so much of the mass media, those outlets see Sanders as dangerously anti-corporate and way too willing to challenge Wall Street, big insurance companies, the fossil fuel industry and the like.

On a political level, the Clinton wing of the party has been running on the equivalent of dumpster-fire fumes since the disastrous loss in November. The party's establishment, entwined with Wall Street and an agenda of continuous military intervention overseas, was just barely able to shoehorn its handpicked choice, Tom Perez, into becoming the new chair of the Democratic National Committee.

In a classic joint interview with MSNBC two months ago, Perez and Sanders showcased just how different their politics are. Perez mumbled platitudes, Sanders was forthright. Perez spoke about victims of an unfair economy, but he refused to denounce or even name their corporate victimizers – while Sanders was glad to do so.

The U.S. media establishment often conflates "populism" of the right and the left, as though Trump and Sanders are somehow symmetrical as anti-establishment figures. And, as in the case of the *New York Times* article that appeared hours after the GOP baseball tragedy, the *Times* has sometimes jumped at the chance to draw far-fetched parallels between Trump's violence-tinged, pseudo-populist messaging from the right and Bernie's humane, inclusive messaging from the left.

Like it or not, the battle over the future of the Democratic Party – including what kind of presidential nominee the party should have in 2020 – is already underway. Overall, the top echelons of corporate media are oriented toward promoting the Clinton wing while denigrating the Bernie wing. The forces that brought us the disastrous 2016 Clinton campaign are not about to give up.

This Is What Pseudo-Democracy Looks Like

December 28, 2017

OLIGARCHY PREVENTS DEMOCRACY. THAT EXPLAINS THE GIST of why the United States became more undemocratic in 2017.

With vast income inequality and corporate power, this country's oligarchy keeps consolidating itself – largely hidden in plain sight – normalized and embossed on the wallpaper of mass-media echo chambers. Several decades of ominous trendlines have brought us to dire tipping points.

"In the American republic the fact of oligarchy is the most dreaded knowledge of all, and our news keeps that knowledge from us," historian Walter Karp wrote. "By their subjugation of the press, the political powers in America have conferred on themselves the greatest of political blessings – Gyges' ring of invisibility." Those words appeared in 1989.

Nearly 30 years later, the power of billionaires, huge banks and Wall Street over U.S. politics is far more dominant, while a propaganda fog diverts attention from their antidemocratic leverage. An array of news media (including big "public" outlets like NPR) and corporate politicians, unwilling to acknowledge let alone challenge the reality of an oligarchy in the United States, love to point accusatory fingers elsewhere.

Days before the end of 2017, I googled the phrase "American oligarchs" and found that it appeared scarcely one-tenth as often as "Russian oligarchs." Yet the gravest injuries and threats to democracy in the USA are overwhelmingly coming from massively capitalized individuals and corporations at the top of the U.S. power structure.

Oligarchs like Sheldon Adelson, Jeff Bezos, Charles Koch, David Koch, Robert Mercer and Rupert Murdoch are wielding enormous power at many levels of the political economy and social zeitgeist, while corporate America functions with expanding latitude and increasing impunity. The extreme concentrations of wealth and economic power are extreme concentrations of political power.

"The fact of oligarchy" that Walter Karp cited at the end of the 1980s now looms larger than ever. In the next few years, reversing the catastrophic momentum will require finding ways to defeat the partisan right arm of oligarchic forces. Noam Chomsky is correct when he calls the present-day Republican Party "the most dangerous organization in world history."

Fighting the GOP right is only part of the imperative. We need an ongoing and escalating grassroots challenge to the national leadership of the Democratic Party, which remains aligned with Wall Street and the warfare state. The tasks ahead involve strengthening progressive populist movements to gain power inside and outside of electoral arenas.

In 2018, whether the races are for U.S. House and Senate seats or for state offices, the path ahead will require fighting for progressive candidates in Democratic primaries and then fighting to defeat Republicans in general elections with Democratic nominees. There will simply be no other way to wrest majority control of Congress away from the Republican Party in the November 2018 election.

The chair of the California Democratic Party's Progressive Caucus, former union organizer Karen Bernal, has a long history of working inside and outside the party. As the author of a section of "Autopsy: The Democratic Party in Crisis" (produced by a task force that I was also part of), she wrote: "Social movements cannot be understood as tools to get Democrats elected. The ebb and flow of social movements offer a rising tide in their own right that along the way can lift Democratic Party candidates – if the party is able to embrace the broad popular sentiment that the movements embody."

The report added: "The Democratic Party is badly positioned to present itself as a foe of the powerful forces causing widespread economic distress for working people, the poor and 'near poor,' the elderly, millennials, people of color – in short, the party's purported base. Weakness of messaging is directly related to the comfort that corporate power enjoys not only in legislative halls across the nation but also within the party itself. Such corporate dominance prevents the party from truthfully projecting itself as an ally of the working class." That must change.

While we see all too clearly how a lack of democracy can – and does – coexist with elections, it is inconceivable that we could have true democracy without elections. They'll be crucial for advancing a progressive agenda to end the undemocratic power of economic elites.

Polls throughout 2017 showed that the most popular politician in the country is Bernie Sanders, who has been denouncing the oligarchy for many years. No wonder the *Washington Post* – owned by the richest person in the world, Jeff Bezos – has gone to centrist extremes to disparage Sanders and what he stands for. The mortal threat to the oligarchy is a sustained groundswell that can propagate genuine democracy.

In late 2017, the main energy for defeating racist anti-immigrant Republican candidates for governor in Virginia and senator in Alabama came from independent grassroots-oriented groups. Notable upsets for legislative seats in a number of states also pointed the way. Community-based organizing is the best avenue for pulling the plug on right-wing politicians.

And that's how we elect people who represent stellar goals for the future. From Tim Keller in Albuquerque, N.M., to Randall Woodfin in Birmingham, Ala., to Steve Schewel in Durham, N.C., genuine progressives became mayors of sizable cities after winning elections in late 2017.

Stoking racism, xenophobia, religious bigotry, anti-gay hatred and hostility to the poor have been major implements in the right-wing tool box that made it possible to elect Trump as president and sustain a Republican majority in Congress. The toxic messaging will surely be augmented by persistent assaults on voting rights. In the last year, the Brennan Center reports, "at least five states – Iowa, Arkansas, North Dakota, Indiana and Georgia – have enacted bills to make it harder for citizens to vote." Such restrictions must be fought with litigation, public education, lobbying, protests and more.

The oligarchy has the power that comes with vast quantities of money. We have the capacity to organize and mobilize people. Democracy is at stake.

In 2018 and beyond, the last thing we need is cynicism that devolves into passivity. What's vital is renewal of energized idealism – with realism about the obstacles to actual democracy and determination to help overcome them.

2018

While the Trump wrecking crew became more accustomed to running the executive and legislative machinery, the leadership of the Democratic Party was mapping out a battle plan for the midterm elections in November. At the same time, a key priority was to thwart the inside threat posed by progressive forces.

The Democratic National Committee was in its second year under chair Tom Perez, who'd won the job in a close election against a Bernie Sanders ally. Some minimal steps gave a bit of ground to progressives, who had shown that they could gain real electoral momentum by nearly wresting the latest presidential nomination away from Hillary Clinton. But Representative Nancy Pelosi and Senator Chuck Schumer, the top Democrats on Capitol Hill, were keeping a firm grip on the party's legislators to deter any progressive efforts of much consequence.

All the while, establishment Democrats were keeping a watchful eye and political guns trained on Bernie Sanders, eager to prevent him from rising again.

BACK TO WORK
UNITED
USA
AMERICA
NOW, WHERE WERE WE ?...
FBI
EPA
INTERIOR
EDUCATION
DEPARTMENT OF STATE
M. WUERKER
POLITICO Andrews McMeel

The "Pelosi Problem" Runs Deep

November 15, 2018

NANCY PELOSI WILL PROBABLY BE THE NEXT HOUSE SPEAKER, a prospect that fills most alert progressives with disquiet, if not dread. But instead of fixating on her as a villain, progressives should recognize the long-standing House Democratic leader as a symptom of a calcified party hierarchy that has worn out its grassroots welcome and is beginning to lose its grip.

Increasingly at odds with the Democratic Party's mobilized base, that grip has held on with gobs of money from centralized, deep-pocket sources – endlessly reinforcing continual deference to corporate power and an ongoing embrace of massively profitable militarism.

Pelosi has earned a reputation as an excellent manager, and she has certainly managed to keep herself in power atop Democrats in the House. She's a deft expert on how Congress works, but she seems out of touch – intentionally or not – with the millions of grassroots progressives who are fed up with her kind of leadership.

Those progressives should not reconcile with Pelosi, any more than they should demonize her. The best course will involve strategic confrontations – nonviolent, emphatic, civilly disobedient – mobilizing the power of protest as well as electoral activism within Democratic primaries.

Such well-planned actions as Tuesday's "Green New Deal" sit-in at Pelosi's Capitol office serve many valuable purposes. (Along the way, they help undermine the absurd right-wing Fox News trope that portrays her as some kind of leftist.) Insistently advocating for strong progressive programs and calling Pelosi out on her actual positions despite nice-sounding rhetoric can effectively widen the range of public debate. Over time, the process creates more space and momentum for a resurgent left.

There is much to counter at the top of the party. Pelosi still refuses to support single-payer enhanced "Medicare for All." As on many other issues, she – and others, such as the more corporate-friendly

House Democratic Whip Steny Hoyer – are clinging to timeworn, Wall Street-friendly positions against powerful political winds generated by years of grassroots activism.

Increasingly, such leadership is isolated from the party it claims to lead. Yet the progressive base is having more and more impact. As a Vox headline proclaimed, more than a year ago, "The stunning Democratic shift on single-payer: In 2008, no leading Democratic presidential candidate backed single-payer. In 2020, all of them might." The Medicare for All Caucus now lists 76 House members.

Any progressive should emphatically reject Pelosi's current embrace of a "pay-go" rule that would straitjacket spending for new social programs by requiring offset tax hikes or budget cuts. Her position is even more outrageous in view of her fervent support for astronomical military spending. Like Senate Minority Leader Chuck Schumer (who was just re-elected to his post), Pelosi went out of her way last winter to proclaim avid support for President Trump's major increase in the already-bloated Pentagon budget, boasting: "In our negotiations, congressional Democrats have been fighting for increases in funding for defense."

Whether our concerns involve militarism, social equity, economic justice, civil liberties, climate change or the overarching necessity of a Green New Deal, the Democratic Party must change from the bottom up. That means progressives across the country should run candidates from precinct levels upward and maintain pressure on all elected officials, including the congressional Democrats with progressive records.

Newly elected House members will raise the total membership of the Congressional Progressive Caucus to about 90. A dozen caucus members are in line to chair House committees in the new Congress; another 30 are set to chair subcommittees. The Progressive Caucus is now co-chaired by Raul Grijalva of Arizona and Mark Pocan of Wisconsin, two of the strongest progressive lawmakers on Capitol Hill. The contrasts between their advocacy and the meanderings of the caucus's more tepid members are sometimes striking.

During the Obama years, by deferring to top-tier party leaders, many in the Progressive Caucus showed themselves to be unreliable advocates for progressive causes when push came to shove – during the 2009 healthcare debate, for example. Yet the left-leaning tendencies in the caucus can now be strengthened and reinforced – if constituent pressure is insistent. When necessary, that insistence should include credible threats of launching primary challenges.

While the governing body of the party, the Democratic National Committee, gave ground this year on such matters as internal party democracy (disempowering superdelegates in the process), senior Democrats have retained a firm hold on such powerful mechanisms as the Democratic Congressional Campaign Committee. It is emblematic of a larger problem that in the run-up to the 2018 midterm elections, an unrelenting series of DCCC emails to millions of recipients featured appeals from such standard party figures as James Carville, Barack Obama, Hillary Clinton, Joe Biden, Adam Schiff, Madeleine Albright, John Kerry, Harry Reid, Nancy Pelosi and Barbara Boxer – none of whom supported Bernie Sanders in the 2016 presidential primaries. The emails reflect how lopsided and corporate the power structures of the DCCC and top-ranking Democrats in Congress remain.

In sync with such corporate sensibilities, some of the party's big mainline names are now mobilizing to pressure incoming Democrats to support Pelosi for speaker. "Democratic Party luminaries are calling members-elect on Pelosi's behalf," *Politico* reported this week; they include New York Gov. Andrew Cuomo, former Vice President Al Gore and former Secretary of State John Kerry.

This year, many progressive individuals and organizations have moved beyond the false choice of either building movements or seriously trying to win elections. We can and must do both – simultaneously, not sequentially – to the benefit of both parallel tasks. The Republican Party's loss of the House was largely due to decisions by substantial numbers of people on the left to engage with the electoral process as never before. Moving forward, we need to strengthen social movements, as well as electoral capacities, so we can end Republican rule and replace it with genuinely progressive governance.

Democratic Party "Leadership" Is Upside Down

November 26, 2018

WHEN DEMOCRATS TAKE CONTROL OF THE HOUSE IN EARLY January, they'll have two kinds of leadership – one from the top of the party's power pyramid, the other from its base. With formal control, Nancy Pelosi and Steny Hoyer can brandish huge carrots and sticks to keep Democratic lawmakers in line. With grassroots support, a growing number of those lawmakers can – and should – strategically step out of line to fight for progressive agendas.

Pelosi and Hoyer have been running the Democratic machinery in the House of Representatives since 2003, and they're experts at combining liberal rhetoric with corporate flackery. Pelosi is frequently an obstacle to advancing progressive proposals. Hoyer is significantly worse as he avidly serves such "constituents" as giant banks, Pentagon contractors and other Wall Street titans. The duo has often functioned as top-drawer power tools in the hands of powerful corporate-military interests.

Pelosi is a longtime wizard at generating and funneling hundreds of millions of election-cycle dollars, and as speaker she'll wield enormous power over committee assignments. But she must keep Democratic House members minimally satisfied – and along the way that should mean yielding more power to the Congressional Progressive Caucus. Buoyed by wins in the midterm elections, the caucus includes two-fifths of all Democrats in the House.

That's where the other kind of leadership comes in – if a hefty number of self-identified progressives in Congress go to the mat to vigorously represent progressive constituencies. For that to happen, a dubious aspect of the Progressive Caucus past must not repeat itself.

"When historic votes come to the House floor, party functionaries are able to whip the Progressive Caucus into compliance," I wrote six years ago. A grim pattern set in during the Obama presidency, "with many Progressive Caucus members making fine statements of vigorous resolve – only to succumb on the House floor under intense pressure from the Obama administration."

Backing down had tragic consequences for the nation's healthcare system. In September 2009, Progressive Caucus leaders sent a letter to President Obama pledging not to vote for any healthcare bill "without a robust public option." They wrote: "Any bill that does not provide, at a minimum, a public option built on the Medicare provider system and with reimbursement based on Medicare rates – not negotiated rates – is unacceptable." Six months later, every member of the Progressive Caucus abandoned the demand and voted for a healthcare bill with no public option at all.

In recent years, the leadership of the Progressive Caucus has become more impressive. The current mix of leaders and new members – which includes veteran lawmaker Raul Grijalva, more recent House arrivals like Mark Pocan, Pramila Jayapal and Ro Khanna, and notable incoming progressives such as Alexandria Ocasio-Cortez, Ilhan Omar, Rashida Tlaib and Ayanna Pressley – seems to augur well.

There are encouraging signs that Congressional Progressive Caucus leaders are using new leverage to gain more power for progressives. After meeting with Pelosi on November 15, Co-Chair Pocan and First Vice-Chair Jayapal released a statement saying "we are pleased that Leader Pelosi shares our commitment to ensuring that CPC members are represented proportionally on the key exclusive committees – including Ways and Means, Energy and Commerce, Appropriations, Financial Services and Intelligence."

Progressive leaders can gain persuasive influence largely because they're advocating for proposals that – as polling verifies – have wide support from the U.S. public, such as a $15-an-hour minimum wage (59 percent), Medicare for All (70 percent), progressive criminal justice reform (65 percent) and higher taxes on the wealthy (76 percent). Behind such political agenda items is an activist base eager to achieve many programs that have been obstructed by most top-ranking Democrats in Congress.

Clearly, much of the Democratic Party's momentum is now coming from the left. And many of the positions that the timeworn Democratic leadership has staked out are now being overrun – outmatched by the cumulative power of dynamic social movements that have generated electoral clout. Medicare for All is a case in point, with numerous likely Democratic presidential candidates climbing on board.

Ultimately, the most profound progressive leadership for Congress isn't in Congress at all. It's in communities and movements across the country – nurturing diverse progressive strengths in many aspects of social change, including at election time.

No matter how intense the top-down pressure gets from Speaker Pelosi, we should insist from the bottom up that members of Congress stand their ground for progressive principles. And – no matter how fervently they embrace the "progressive" label – if congressmembers aren't willing to fight for those principles, then the grassroots should mobilize: to create an outcry, to lobby and to consider launching primary challenges. No elected officials should be immune from scrutiny and accountability.

2019

With the 2018 midterm elections completed – Democrats had regained the House – a large cast of political characters was off and running for the party's president nomination. Senators Bernie Sanders and Elizabeth Warren were at the left edge, while more than a dozen other candidates also jostled for media attention and momentum. Chief among them was former Vice President Joe Biden.

The corporate media knives were out early and often for Sanders. And so, the "news" about his campaign for the 2020 nomination soon took on a déjà vu quality, resuming the kind of negative coverage that had typified much of the spin in 2016 – when, as the media watch group FAIR documented early that year, "the *Washington Post* ran 16 negative stories on Bernie Sanders in 16 hours."

The strength of the Sanders campaign set off loud alarms in many bastions of corporate power. And when Biden seemed to falter, blue-chip investors began to look seriously for another candidate who might serve as a reliable substitute for him as the 2020 standard-bearer.

THE DEMO DERBY ROUNDS THE BEND

Bernie 2020 Campaign Has Corporate Democrats Running Scared

February 12, 2019

WITH A LAUNCH OF THE BERNIE SANDERS 2020 CAMPAIGN ON the near horizon, efforts to block his trajectory to the Democratic presidential nomination are intensifying. The lines of attack are already aggressive – and often contradictory.

One media meme says that Bernie has made so much headway in moving the Democratic Party leftward that he's no longer anything special. We're supposed to believe that candidates who've adjusted their sails to the latest political wind are just as good as the candidate who generated the wind in the first place.

Bloomberg News supplied the typical spin in a February 8 article headlined "Sanders Risks Getting Crowded Out in 2020 Field of Progressives." The piece laid out the narrative: "Sanders may find himself a victim of his own success in driving the party to the left with his 2016 run. The field of Democratic presidential hopefuls includes at least a half-dozen candidates who've adopted in whole or in part the platform that helped Sanders build a loyal following . . ."

Yet Bernie is also being targeted as too marginal. The same *Bloomberg* article quoted Howard Dean, a long-ago liberal favorite who has become a hawkish lobbyist and corporate mouthpiece "There will be hardcore, hard left progressives who will have nobody but Bernie, but there won't be many."

So, is Bernie now too much like other Democratic presidential candidates, or is he too much of an outlier? In the mass media, both seem to be true. In the real world, neither are true.

Last week, *Business Insider* reported on new polling about Bernie's proposal "to increase the estate tax, the tax paid by heirs on assets passed down by the deceased. Sanders' idea would lower the threshold to qualify for the tax to $3.5 million in assets, down from the current $11 million. The plan would also introduce a graduating scale of tax rates for the estates of wealthier Americans, eventually reaching a 77 percent marginal rate for assets over $1 billion."

Here are the poll results: "When presented with the details of the proposal, 37 percent of respondents supported Sanders' policy while 26 percent opposed, according to Insider's survey." (The rest had no opinion.)

That kind of response from the public is a far cry from claims that Sanders is somehow fringe. In fact, the ferocity of media attacks on him often indicates that corporate power brokers are afraid his strong progressive populism is giving effective voice to majority views of the public.

A vast range of grassroots organizing – outside and inside of electoral arenas – has created the current leftward momentum. "As a progressive, it is heartening to see so many other candidates voice support for Senator Sanders' policies," said Alan Minsky, executive director at Progressive Democrats of America. "However, I've been around the block enough times to know that politicians who adopt positions in tune with the fashion of the moment are not as trustworthy as those rare few, like Bernie Sanders, who have held firm to a powerful social justice vision through his entire long career."

I also asked for a comment from Pia Gallegos, former chair of the Adelante Progressive Caucus of the New Mexico Democratic Party. "Bernie's competitors lack his track record on economic security for all American workers, Medicare for All, free public college education, taxing the rich and opposing bloated military budgets," she said. "Those are long-standing positions that – more than ever – resonate with grassroots activists and voters. Other Democratic presidential candidates will try to imitate this populist agenda, but only Bernie can speak with the vision, clarity and moral authority that the Democratic Party's presidential candidate needs to defeat the incumbent."

The overarching fear that defenders of oligarchy have about Bernie Sanders is not that he's out of step with most Americans – it's that he's in step with them. For corporate elites determined to retain undemocratic power, a successful Bernie 2020 campaign would be the worst possible outcome of the election.

Joe Biden on the Relaunch Pad: He's Worse Than You Thought

March 11, 2019

WHEN THE *NEW YORK TIMES* FRONT-PAGED ITS LATEST ANTI-left polemic masquerading as a news article, the March 9 piece declared: "Should former Vice President Joseph R. Biden Jr. enter the race, as his top advisers vow he soon will, he would have the best immediate shot at the moderate mantle."

On the verge of relaunching, Joe Biden is poised to come to the rescue of the corporate political establishment – at a time when, in the words of the *Times*, "the sharp left turn in the Democratic Party and the rise of progressive presidential candidates are unnerving moderate Democrats." After 36 years in the Senate and eight as vice president, Biden is by far the most seasoned servant of corporate power with a prayer of becoming the next president.

When Biden read this paragraph in a recent *Politico* article, his ears must have been burning: "Early support from deep-pocketed financial executives could give Democrats seeking to break out of the pack an important fundraising boost. But any association with bankers also opens presidential hopefuls to sharp attacks from an ascendant left."

The direct prey of Biden's five-decade "association with bankers" include millions of current and former college students now struggling under avalanches of debt; they can thank Biden for his prodigious services to the lending industry. Andrew Cockburn identifies an array of victims in his devastating profile of Biden in the March issue of *Harper's* magazine. For instance:

- "Biden was long a willing foot soldier in the campaign to emasculate laws allowing debtors relief from loans they cannot repay. As far back as 1978, he helped negotiate a deal rolling back bankruptcy protections for graduates with federal student loans, and in 1984 worked to do the same for borrowers with loans for vocational schools."

- "Even when the ostensible objective lay elsewhere, such as drug-related crime, Biden did not forget his banker friends. Thus the 1990 Crime Control Act, with Biden as chief sponsor, further limited debtors' ability to take advantage of bankruptcy protections."

• Biden worked diligently to strengthen the hand of credit-card firms against consumers. At the same time, "the credit card giant MBNA was Biden's largest contributor for much of his Senate career, while also employing his son Hunter as an executive and, later, as a well-remunerated consultant."

Media mythology about "Lunch Bucket Joe" cannot stand up to scrutiny. His bona fides as a pal of working people are about as solid and believable as those of the last Democratic nominee for president.

But Biden's fealty to corporate power has been only one aspect of his many-faceted record that progressives will widely find repugnant to the extent they learn about it.

Since the #MeToo movement began, some retrospective media coverage has assessed Biden's highly problematic role in chairing the Clarence Thomas - Anita Hill hearings of the Senate Judiciary Committee. And in recent days, *Washington Post* reporting has brought into focus his backstory of pandering to white racism against African-Americans during much of his Senate career.

As a 32-year-old senator, in 1975, Biden commented: "I do not buy the concept, popular in the '60s, which said, 'We have suppressed the black man for 300 years and the white man is now far ahead in the race for everything our society offers. In order to even the score, we must now give the black man a head start, or even hold the white man back, to even the race.' I don't buy that."

More attention is also needed to Biden's role as Judiciary Committee chair pushing through the now-notorious landmark 1994 crime bill. In the process of championing the bill, Biden warned of "predators on our streets" during a 1993 speech on the Senate floor.

"It doesn't matter whether or not they were deprived as a youth," Biden proclaimed. "It doesn't matter whether or not they had no background that enabled them to become socialized into the fabric of society. It doesn't matter whether or not they're the victims of society. The end result is they're about to knock my mother on the head with a lead pipe, shoot my sister, beat up my wife, take on my sons."

Now, a new Iowa poll shows Biden and Bernie Sanders neck and neck in the first-in-the-nation contest for the nomination, with the rest of the candidates far behind in the state. For quite a while, Biden has been sharpening his hatchet to swing at progressive populism in general – and Bernie in particular.

In typical Biden style, the former vice president is eager to stake out the middle of the road, between ultra-predatory capitalism and solidarity with working-class people. At an October 2017 gathering in Alabama, he said: "Guys, the wealthy are as patriotic as the poor. I know Bernie doesn't like me saying that, but they are." Later, Biden elaborated on the theme when he told an audience at the Brookings Institution, "I don't think five hundred billionaires are the reason we're in trouble. The folks at the top aren't bad guys."

As Branko Marcetic pointed out in *Jacobin* last summer, "at a time when left-wing populism is increasingly accepted as the antidote to Trump and the GOP's nativist and corporate-friendly pitch, Biden stands as a remnant of precisely the sort of left-averse, triangulating Democratic politics that Hillary Clinton was relentlessly criticized for personifying."

Biden makes clear his distaste for the current progressive populist wave. "I know some want to single out big corporations for all the blame," he wrote in a blog post. "It is true that the balance has shifted too much in favor of corporations and against workers. But consumers, workers, and leaders have the power to hold every corporation to a higher standard, not simply cast business as the enemy or let industry off the hook."

One of the many industries that Biden has a long record of letting "off the hook" is the war business. In that mode, Biden did more than any other Democratic senator to greenlight the March 2003 invasion of Iraq.

It wasn't just that Biden voted for the Iraq war on the Senate floor five months before it began. During the lead-up to that vote, in August 2002, as chairman of the Foreign Relations Committee, he presided over sham hearings – refusing to allow experts who opposed an invasion to get any words in edgewise – while a cavalcade of war hawks testified in the national spotlight.

"It is difficult to over-estimate the critical role Biden played in making the tragedy of the Iraq war possible," Middle East studies professor Stephen Zunes wrote. "More than two months prior to the 2002 war resolution even being introduced, in what was widely interpreted as the first sign that Congress would endorse a U.S. invasion of Iraq, Biden declared on August 4 that the United States was probably going to war. In his powerful position as chair of the Senate Foreign Relations Committee, he orchestrated a propaganda show designed to sell the war to skeptical colleagues and the America public by ensuring that dissenting voices would not get a fair hearing."

Joe Biden's friendly TV persona appeals to many. He smiles well and has a gift of gab. Most political journalists in the mass media like him. He's an apt frontrunner for the military-industry complex and the corporate power structure that it serves. Whether Biden can win the 2020 Democratic presidential nomination will largely depend on how many voters don't know much about his actual record.

Bernie Is Not a Wind Sock

March 26, 2019

BERNIE SANDERS WRAPPED UP A WEEKEND CAMPAIGN SWING through California with a Sunday afternoon speech to 16,000 of us a few miles from the Golden Gate Bridge. News coverage seemed unlikely to convey much about the event. The multiracial crowd reflected the latest polling that shows great diversity of support for Bernie, contrary to corporate media spin. High energy for basic social change was in the air.

Speaking from the podium, Bernie 2020 co-chair Nina Turner asked and answered a question about the campaign: "What's love got to do with it? Everything."

Those words made me think of a little-known statement by Martin Luther King Jr., as vitally true in 2019 as in 1967. "Now, we got to get this thing right," he said. "What is needed is a realization that power without love is reckless and abusive, and that love without power is sentimental and anemic. Power at its best is love implementing the demands of justice, and justice at its best is love correcting everything that stands against love."

And so, Dr. King was saying, love and power need each other. Just one or the other just won't do. Combining the two is essential. That's a way to understand what Turner said at the rally in San Francisco: "This is a moment of transcendence."

The Sanders campaign is a nationwide struggle for the kind of power that King extolled as "love implementing the demands of justice." In his words, "Power properly understood is nothing but the ability to achieve purpose."

The Sanders campaign is a political opportunity unlike any we've seen in our lifetimes. With profound purpose, it raises the stakes to fit the magnitude of what is at stake; it challenges in national electoral terms the kind of destructive domination that has ruled with dispiriting and deadly results. "We're going to have to fight Wall Street, neoliberals, those who don't want the change to come," Turner said.

Alone among the candidates for the 2020 Democratic presidential nomination, Bernie Sanders has always been part of progressive movements. The only way that the campaign can overcome corporate media, Wall Street and other power centers of the establishment will be with massive bottom-up mobilization in communities across the country. As Bernie said on Sunday, "We are going to put together an unprecedented grassroots campaign."

A current media meme – ignoring the importance of Bernie's long-standing record – assumes that he is likely to lose many votes to other candidates who've recently endorsed his 2016 campaign proposals.

But it matters greatly that Bernie has unique credibility as someone who has been part of progressive social movements during the last several decades – and who hasn't waited for opinions to become fashionable before expressing them.

"It's hard not to be a bit wary of people who know how the wind is blowing and now are blowing with it," I told a *San Francisco Chronicle* reporter who quoted me in an article that appeared hours before the rally. "Bernie is part of movements that create the wind. Bernie is not a wind sock."

For decades, Bernie has been tirelessly advocating for Medicare for All single-payer healthcare. In the last few years or months, some of his opponents have come around to voice often-equivocal support. The credibility of commitment is vastly different. When Sanders declared for the umpteenth time at the San Francisco rally that "healthcare is a human right," no one could doubt that he really meant it.

Similarly, Bernie has long been calling for drastic new policies to push back against climate change. He voiced concerns about a warming planet as early as the 1980s.

Overall, a vast number of issues fall under a clear approach that Bernie has long stated, as he did on Sunday: "We say no to oligarchy, yes to democracy."

Bernie's speech in San Francisco included clarity on some issues that has become sharper than ever, as in his denunciations of the prison-industrial complex, the cruel injustice of cash bail and systemic racism. And at last, as a presidential candidate, he is calling out by name "the military-industrial complex."

Declaring that he aims for a presidency to challenge the bloated military budget, Bernie said: "We are not going to invest in never-ending wars." It was a statement that caused some of the loudest cheering of the afternoon, along with chants of "No more wars!" As those chants subsided, he said: "I know it's not easy, but our job is to lead the world away from war and invest in human needs."

Bernie called for breaking up the big banks. And he addressed the power of the pharmaceutical and insurance industries: "When we talk about lowering prescription drug costs and moving to Medicare for All, we have got to recognize, we have a battle in front of us. These guys will spend endless amounts of money. Will you stand with me and take on the drug companies and the insurance companies?"

And he went on: "If we're going to protect family-based agriculture from Vermont to California, we have got to stand up to agribusiness. We have got to stand up to the prison-industrial complex. We've got to stand up to the fossil fuel industry. In other words, it's easy enough for somebody to give you a speech about all the things he or she wants to do. But those changes do not take place unless people stand up and fight back. And that is what this campaign is about."

When Bernie finished his speech, a woman stepped to the microphone with a guitar and began to play some familiar chords. Bernie returned to the mic to quickly say: "This is Sarah Guthrie, granddaughter of Woody Guthrie."

And she began to sing:

As I was walking that ribbon of highway

I saw above me that endless skyway

I saw below me the golden valley

This land was made for you and me

Moments later, Sarah Guthrie sang a version of a verse that has been rarely heard:

There was a great high wall

That tried to stop me

And on the wall said "No Trespassing"

But on the other side

It didn't say nothing

That side was made for you and me

Why Bernie Sanders Is Correct About the *Washington Post* – and Corporate Media Overall

August 14, 2019

MANY DECADES AGO, THE GREAT MEDIA CRITIC GEORGE SELDES observed: "The most sacred cow of the press is the press itself." That remains true today.

Bernie Sanders set off the latest round of outraged denial from elite media this week when he talked to a crowd in New Hampshire about the tax avoidance of Amazon (which did not pay any federal income tax last year). Sanders went on to say: "I wonder why the *Washington Post* – which is owned by Jeff Bezos, who owns Amazon – doesn't write particularly good articles about me. I don't know why. But I guess maybe there's a connection."

Sanders has fought explicitly and effectively to raise the wages of Amazon workers as well as millions of others. Yet the mass-media pretense is that the financial interests of the *Post*'s owner have no effect on the newspaper's coverage of Sanders.

Corporate denial is the name of that media game. Usually, expressed denials aren't necessary. But there's nothing usual about Bernie Sanders, who's been willing to call out the biases and blind spots of corporate media since he entered politics.

For his latest transgression, Sanders earned purportedly authoritative pushback from the likes of the *Post*'s top editor, its media columnist and others with high media visibility. "Contrary to the conspiracy theory the senator seems to favor," *Post* executive editor Martin Baron declared, "Jeff Bezos allows our newsroom to operate with full independence, as our reporters and editors can attest."

The *Post*'s media columnist Margaret Sullivan quickly chimed in with a harmonizing tweet on Tuesday, defending her editor boss along with the owner of the paper: "I've never seen or heard a hint of @jeffbezos interfering in @washingtonpost coverage."

CNN's Chris Cillizza, citing his work at the newspaper for a decade, indignantly wrote: "For the last three of my years at the *Post*, Bezos owned the company. Not once in all of that time – and I wrote multiple pieces a day about politics and politicians (including Sanders and Trump) over that time – was there ever even a whiff of Bezos' influence in the newsroom."

As George Seldes commented long ago, "The most stupid boast in the history of present-day journalism is that of the writer who says, 'I have never been given orders; I am free to do as I like.'" Seldes noted that reporters routinely "know from contact with the great minds of the press lords or from the simple deduction that the bosses are in big business and the news must be slanted accordingly, or from the general intangible atmosphere which prevails everywhere, what they can do and what they must never do."

All Baron or Sullivan would need to do to disprove their own current claims would be to write a bunch of pieces denouncing the man who owns the *Post* – and then see what happens due to their breach of required self-censorship.

On television, a CNN anchor joined with a *USA Today* columnist to claim that Sanders's criticism of the *Post*'s coverage was free of evidence. The fact that corporate-media employees are vehemently defending corporate media is illustrative of the dynamic. It makes you wonder where career self-interest ends and sincere delusion begins.

Baron, Sullivan, Cillizza and countless other employees of corporate media are well-paid while publicly maintaining their denial in the service of corporate power. So, with the virtues of the *Washington Post* on parade, Emperor Bezos must be decked out in the journalistic finery of his new clothes, even when the self-interest and implications of billionaire leverage over media are stark naked.

What Bernie Sanders is pointing out is not – and he never said it was – a "conspiracy." The problems are much deeper and more pernicious, having to do with the financial structures of media institutions that enable profit-driven magnates and enormous corporations to dominate the flow of news and commentary.

This year, the *Post* has strained to throw negative light on Sanders's campaign, whether focusing on Wall Street or Venezuela. Nor is the *Post* far afield from other powerful media outlets. For instance, the *New York Times* reportage has taken Sanders to task for alleged sins such as desiring to exercise control over his own campaign and failing to please Democratic critics who are actually corporate lobbyists but not identified as such.

Nor is the AT&T-owned CNN far afield from the baseline of cable news giants that supposedly provide a liberal alternative to the odious Fox News. Coverage from MSNBC – owned by Comcast, "the world's largest entertainment company" – has provoked one assessment after another after another documenting the network's anti-Bernie bias.

"The corporate-owned and corporate-advertiser-funded media of this country are the biggest barriers between Bernie Sanders and the Oval Office," I wrote five months ago. "Often functioning as propaganda outlets, the major news media serve as an amplification system for corporate power that has long shielded the Democratic Party from the combined 'threats' of social movements and progressive populist candidates."

Journalists who have staked their careers on remaining in the good graces of corporate employers are certainly inclined to say in public that billionaire owners and huge corporations don't constrain their journalistic work. And in their minds, they might be telling the truth. As George Orwell wrote, "Circus dogs jump when the trainer cracks his whip, but the really well-trained dog is the one that turns his somersault when there is no whip."

The Primary Contradiction: Corporate Power vs. Progressive Populism

August 29, 2019

FOR PLUTOCRATS, THIS SUMMER HAS GOTTEN A BIT SCARY. TWO feared candidates are rising. Trusted candidates are underperforming. The 2020 presidential election could turn out to be a real-life horror movie: A Nightmare on Wall Street.

"Wall Street executives who want Trump out," *Politico* reported in January, "list a consistent roster of appealing nominees that includes former Vice President Joe Biden and Senators Cory Booker of New Jersey, Kirsten Gillibrand of New York and Kamala Harris of California."

But seven months later, those "appealing nominees" don't seem appealing to a lot of voters. Biden's frontrunner status is looking shaky, while other Wall Street favorites no longer inspire investor confidence: Harris is stuck in single digits, Booker is several points below her, and Gillibrand just dropped out of the race.

Meanwhile, Bernie Sanders and Elizabeth Warren are drawing large crowds and rising in polls. In pivotal early states like Iowa and especially New Hampshire, reputable poll averages indicate that Biden is scarcely ahead.

"Bankers' biggest fear" is that "the nomination goes to an anti-Wall Street crusader" like Warren or Sanders, *Politico* reported, quoting the CEO of a "giant bank" who said: "It can't be Warren and it can't be Sanders. It has to be someone centrist and someone who can win."

But the very biggest fear among corporate elites is that Warren or Sanders *could win* – and then use the presidency to push back against oligarchy. If Biden can't be propped up, there's no candidate looking strong enough to stop them.

Biden, Warren and Sanders, as the *New York Times* reported on Wednesday, are "a threesome that seems to have separated from the rest of the primary field." In fourth place, national polling averages show, Harris is far behind.

Biden's distinguished record of servicing corporate America spans five decades. He is eager to continue that work from the Oval Office, but can he get there? A week ago, a *Times* headline noted reasons for doubt: "Joe Biden's Poll Numbers Mask an Enthusiasm Challenge." Enthusiasm for Biden has been high among Democratic-aligned elites, but not among Democratic-aligned voters.

While corporate news organizations – and corporate-enmeshed "public" outlets like NPR News and the "PBS NewsHour" – evade primary contradictions, Sanders directly hammers at how huge corporations are propelling media bias and undermining democracy.

Even though he has inspired media onslaughts – such as the now-notorious 16 anti-Sanders articles published by the *Washington Post* in a pivotal 16-hour period during the 2016 primary contest – the Sanders campaign is so enormous that even overtly hostile outlets must give him some space. In an op-ed piece he wrote that the *Post* published seven weeks ago, Sanders confronted Biden's wealth-fondling approach.

Under the headline "The Straightest Path to Racial Equality Is Through the One Percent," Sanders quoted a statement from Biden: "I don't think 500 billionaires are the reason why we're in trouble." Sanders responded, "I respectfully disagree" – and he went on to say: "It is my view that any presidential candidate who claims to believe that black lives matter has to take on the institutions that have continually exploited black lives."

Such insight about systemic exploitation is sacrilege to the secular faith of wealth accumulation that touts reaching billionaire status as a kind of divine ascension. Yet Sanders boldly challenges that kind of hollowness, shedding a fierce light on realities of corporate capitalism.

"Structural problems require structural solutions," Sanders pointed out in his *Post* article, "and promises of mere 'access' have never guaranteed black Americans equality in this country.... 'Access' to healthcare is an empty promise when you can't afford high premiums, co-pays or deductibles. And an 'opportunity' for an equal education is an opportunity in name only when you can't afford to live in a good school district or to pay college tuition. Jobs, healthcare, criminal justice and education are linked, and progress will not be made unless we address the economic systems that oppress Americans at their root."

Like many other progressives, I continue to actively support Sanders as a candidate who bypasses euphemisms, names ultra-powerful villains – and directly challenges those in power who've been warping and gaming the economic systems against working-class people.

Those systems are working quite nicely for the ultra-rich, like the giant bank CEO who told *Politico* that "it can't be Warren and it can't be Sanders." That's the decision from Wall Street. The decision from Main Street is yet to be heard.

The Crass Warfare of Billionaires Against Sanders and Warren

November 7, 2019

FOR MANY DECADES, ANY POLITICIAN DARING TO FIGHT FOR economic justice was liable to be denounced for engaging in "class warfare." It was always a grimly laughable accusation, coming from wealthy elites as well as their functionaries in corporate media and elective office. In the real world, class warfare – or whatever you want to call it – has always been an economic and political reality.

In recent decades, class war in the USA has become increasingly lopsided. The steady decline in union membership, the worsening of income inequality and the hollowing out of the public sector have been some results of ongoing assaults on social decency and countess human lives. Corporate power has run amuck.

Now, the billionaire class is worried. For the first time in memory, there's a real chance that the next president could threaten the very existence of billionaires – or at least significantly reduce their uncon-scionable rate of wealth accumulation – in a country and on a planet with so much human misery due to extreme economic disparities.

In early fall, when Bernie Sanders said "I don't think that billion-aires should exist," many billionaires heard an existential threat. It was hardly a one-off comment; the Bernie 2020 campaign followed up with national distribution of a bumper sticker saying "Billionaires should not exist."

When Elizabeth Warren stands on a debate stage and argues for a targeted marginal tax on the astronomically rich, such advocacy is anathema to those who believe that the only legitimate class war is the kind waged from the top down. In early autumn, CNBC reported that "Democratic donors on Wall Street and in big business are preparing to sit out the presidential campaign fundraising cycle – or even back President Donald Trump – if Senator Elizabeth Warren wins the party's nomination."

As for Bernie Sanders – less than four years after he carried every county in West Virginia against Hillary Clinton in the presidential primary – the state's Democratic Senator Joe Manchin flatly declared last week that if Sanders wins the nomination, he would not vote for his party's nominee against Trump in November 2020.

Some billionaires support Trump and some don't. But few billionaires have a good word to say about Sanders or Warren. And the pattern of billionaires backing their Democratic rivals is illuminating.

"Dozens of American billionaires have pulled out their checkbooks to support candidates engaged in a wide-open battle for the Democratic presidential nomination," *Forbes* reported this summer. The dollar total of those donations given directly to a campaign (which federal law limits to $2,800 each) is less significant than the sentiment they reflect. And people with huge wealth are able to dump hundreds of thousands or even millions of dollars at once into a Super PAC, which grassroots-parched AstroTurf candidate Joe Biden greenlighted last month.

The donations from billionaires to the current Democratic candidates could be viewed as a kind of Oligarchy Confidence Index, based on data from the Federal Election Commission. As reported by *Forbes*, Pete Buttigieg leads all the candidates with 23 billionaire donors, followed by 18 for Cory Booker, and 17 for Kamala Harris. Among the other candidates who have qualified for the debate coming up later this month, Biden has 13 billionaire donors and Amy Klobuchar has 8, followed by 3 for Elizabeth Warren, 1 for Tulsi Gabbard, and 1 for Andrew Yang. Meanwhile, Bernie Sanders has zero billionaire donors.

(The tenth person who has qualified for the next debate, self-funding billionaire candidate Tom Steyer, is in a class by himself.)

Meanwhile, relying on contributions from small donors, Sanders and Warren "eagerly bait, troll and bash billionaires at every opportunity," in the words of a recent *Los Angeles Times* news story. "They send out missives to donors boasting how much damage their plans would inflict on the wallets of specific wealthy families and corporations."

The newspaper added: "Sanders boasts that his wealth tax would cost Amazon owner Jeff Bezos $8.9 billion per year. He even championed a bill with the acronym BEZOS: The Stop Bad Employers By Zeroing Out Subsidies Act would have forced Amazon and other large firms to pay the full cost of food stamps and other benefits received by their lowest-wage employees."

For extremely rich people who confuse net worth with human worth, the prospect of losing out on billions is an outrageous possibility. And so, a few months ago, Facebook mega-billionaire Mark Zuckerberg expressed his antipathy toward Warren while meeting with employees. As a transcript of leaked audio makes clear, Warren's vision of using anti-trust laws to break up Big Tech virtual monopolies was more than Facebook's head could stand to contemplate.

"But look," Zuckerberg said, "at the end of the day, if someone's going to try to threaten something that existential, you go to the mat and you fight."

The fight happening now for the Democratic presidential nomination largely amounts to class warfare. And the forces that have triumphed in the past are outraged that they currently have to deal with so much progressive opposition. As Carl von Clausewitz observed, "A conqueror is always a lover of peace."

2020

The economic populism of the Sanders campaign continued to catch fire during the first months of 2020, while many forces teamed up to function as fire extinguishers. The Democratic Party establishment did what it could to smother the grassroots blaze.

Joe Biden's embarrassing fifth-place finish in the New Hampshire primary, with just 8 percent of the vote, put his campaign on proverbial life-support. But rescue came 18 days later from South Carolina, at the end of February, when Biden won a landslide victory in the state's primary. After the win, several candidates responded to pressure by quickly dropping out of the race and effusively endorsing him.

From there, Biden was on a mainstream roll. And the deadly spread of Covid in early spring impeded the Sanders campaign's ability to push back with more of its activist dynamism on the ground. After Biden clinched the nomination, progressives largely closed ranks behind him because of the overarching need to prevent Trump from winning re-election. Biden squeaked through.

MEDICARE FOR ALL!
FREE COLLEGE!
NO WARS
LEGAL POT!
REVOLUTION
Bernie
Polite Pragmatism
RETURN TO Status Quo!
Incremental Change!
Change
I JUST DON'T GET IT.
M.WUERKER
POLITICO
Andrews McMeel

The Escalating Class War Against Bernie Sanders

February 17, 2020

MORE THAN EVER, BERNIE SANDERS IS PUBLIC ENEMY NUMBER one for power elites that thrive on economic injustice. The Bernie 2020 campaign is a direct threat to the undemocratic leverage that extremely wealthy individuals and huge corporations constantly exert on the political process. No wonder we're now seeing so much anti-Bernie rage from leading corporate Democrats – eagerly amplified by corporate media. In American politics, hell hath no fury like corporate power scorned.

Flagrant media biases against Sanders are routine in a wide range of mainstream outlets. (The media watch group FAIR has long documented the problem, illuminated by one piece after another after another after another just this month.) In sharp contrast, positivity toward Sanders in mass media spheres is scarce.

The pattern is enmeshed with the corporatism that the Sanders campaign seeks to replace with genuine democracy – disempowering great wealth and corporate heft while empowering everyday people to participate in a truly democratic process.

Big media are continually amplifying the voices of well-paid reporters and pundits whose jobs involve acceptance of corporate power, including the prerogatives of corporate owners and sponsors. And, in news coverage of politics, there's an inexhaustible supply of former Democratic officeholders and appointees who've been lucratively feeding from corporate troughs as lobbyists, consultants and PR operatives. Their corporate ties usually go unmentioned.

An important media headquarters for hostility toward the Sanders campaign is MSNBC, owned by Comcast – a notoriously anti-labor and anti-consumer corporation. "People need to remember," I pointed out on *Democracy Now!*, "that if you, for instance, don't trust Comcast, why would you trust a network that is owned by Comcast? These are class interests being worked out where the top strata of ownership and investors hires the CEO, hires the managing editors, hires the reporters. And so, what we're seeing, and not to be rhetorical about it, but we really are seeing a class war underway."

Routinely, the talking heads and go-to sources for mainline news outlets are far removed from the economic pressures besetting so many Americans. And so, media professionals with the most clout and largest megaphones are quite distant from the Sanders base.

Voting patterns in the New Hampshire primary reflected whose economic interests the Sanders campaign is promising to serve. With 10 active candidates on the Democratic ballot, Sanders "won 4 in 10 of voters with household incomes under $50,000 and nearly 3 in 10 with incomes between $50,00 and $99,000," the *Washington Post* reported.

Meanwhile, a trio of researchers associated with the Institute for New Economic Thinking – Thomas Ferguson, Jie Chen and Paul Jorgensen – found that "the higher the town's income, the fewer votes cast" for Sanders. "Lower income towns in New Hampshire voted heavily for Sanders; richer towns did the opposite." The researchers saw in the data "further dramatic evidence of a point we have made before: that the Democratic Party is now sharply divided by social class."

It's a reality with media implications that are hidden in plain sight. The often-vitriolic and sometimes preposterous attacks on Sanders via powerful national media outlets are almost always coming from affluent or outright wealthy people. Meanwhile, low-income Americans have virtually zero access to the TV studios (other than providing after-hours janitorial services).

With very few exceptions, the loudest voices to be heard from mass media are coming from individuals with wealth far above the financial vicinity of average Americans. Virtually none of the most widely read, seen and heard journalists are on the low end of the nation's extreme income inequality. Viewed in that light – and keeping in mind that corporate ownership and advertising dominate mainstream media – it shouldn't be surprising that few prominent journalists have much good to say about a presidential campaign fiercely aligned with the working class.

"If there is going to be class warfare in this country," Bernie Sanders told the Iowa AFL-CIO convention last summer, "it's time that the working class of this country won that war and not just the corporate elite." To the corporate elite, goals like that are unacceptable.

As a Corporate Tool, Buttigieg Is Now a Hammer to Bash Sanders

February 24, 2020

SOON AFTER HIS DISTANT THIRD-PLACE FINISH IN THE NEVADA caucuses, Pete Buttigieg sent out a mass email saying that "Senator Sanders believes in an inflexible, ideological revolution that leaves out most Democrats, not to mention most Americans." The blast depicted "the choice before us" in stark terms: "We can prioritize either ideological purity or inclusive victory. We can either call people names online or we can call them into our movement. We can either tighten a narrow and hardcore base or open the tent to a new, broad, big-hearted American coalition."

The bizarre accusations of being "narrow" and not "inclusive" were aimed at a candidate who'd just won a historic victory with one of the broadest coalitions in recent Democratic Party history.

Buttigieg has gone from pseudo-progressive to anti-progressive in the last year, and much of his current mission involves denouncing Bernie Sanders with attack lines that are corporate-media favorites ("ideological purity… call people names online… a narrow and hardcore base"). Buttigieg's chances of winning the 2020 presidential nomination are now tiny, but he might have a bright future as a rising leader of corporate Democrats.

Weirdly, Buttigieg's claim that Sanders has "a narrow and hardcore base" came from someone who appears to be almost incapable of getting votes from black people. In Nevada, columnist E.J. Dionne noted, Buttigieg "received virtually no African American votes." And Buttigieg made his claim in the midst of a Nevada vote count showing that Sanders received more than three times as many votes as he did. The *Washington Post* reported that Sanders "even narrowly prevailed among those who identified as moderate or conservative."

As chances that Buttigieg could win the nomination slip away – the latest polling in South Carolina indicates his vote total there on Saturday is unlikely to be any higher than it was in Nevada – his mission is being steadily repurposed. After increasingly aligning himself with the dominant corporate sectors of the party – vacuuming up millions of dollars in bundled checks along the way – Buttigieg is hurling an array of bogus accusations at Sanders.

Four months ago, while Buttigieg's poll numbers were spiking in Iowa and big donations from wealthy donors poured in, I wrote an article with a headline dubbing him a "Sharp Corporate Tool." The piece cited an influx of contributions to Buttigieg from the health insurance, pharmaceutical and hospital industries – while he executed a U-turn from proclaiming support for Medicare for All to touting a deceptive rhetorical concoction called "Medicare for all who want it." I concluded that Buttigieg is "a glib ally of corporate America posing as an advocate for working people and their families."

Since then, continuing his rightward swerve, Buttigieg has become even more glib, refining his campaign's creation myth and fine-tuning his capacity to combine corporate policy positions with wispy intimations of technocratic populism. Buttigieg is highly articulate, very shrewd – and now, in attack mode, more valuable than ever to corporate patrons who are feverishly trying to figure out how to prevent Sanders from winning the nomination. During last week's Nevada debate, Buttigieg warned that Sanders "wants to burn this party down."

Over the weekend, the Buttigieg campaign sent out email that tried to obscure its major support from extremely wealthy backers. "At the last debate," Buttigieg's deputy campaign manager Hari Sevugan wrote indignantly, "Senator Bernie Sanders condemned us for taking contributions from billionaires. That's interesting. Because what that tells us is in the eyes of Bernie Sanders, the donations of 45 folks (that's .0054% of our total donor base) are more important than the donations of nearly 1,000,000 grassroots supporters."

But Sevugan left out the pivotal roles that very rich contributors have played in launching and sustaining the Buttigieg campaign, with lobbyists and corporate executives serving as high-dollar collectors of bundled donations that add up to untold millions. Buttigieg's corresponding shifts in policy prescriptions make some sense if we follow the money.

In a detailed article that appeared last week, "Buttigieg Is a Wall Street Democrat Beholden to Corporate Interests," former Communications Workers of America chief economist Kenneth Peres summed up:

"Buttigieg and his supporters like to portray him as a 'change agent.' However, he has proven to be a change agent that will not in any significant way challenge the current distribution of power, wealth and income in this country. Given his history, it is no surprise that Wall Street, Big Tech, Big Pharma, Health Insurers, Real Estate Developers and Private Equity have decided to invest millions of dollars into Buttigieg's campaign."

In the aftermath of the Nevada caucuses, Buttigieg is escalating his attacks on Sanders, in sync with "news" coverage that is especially virulent from some major corporate outlets. Consider, for example, the de facto smear article that the *New York Times* printed on Sunday. Or the venomous hostility toward Sanders that's routine on Comcast-owned MSNBC, which has stepped up its routine trashing of Sanders by journalists and invited guests.

More than ever, corporate Democrats and their media allies are freaking out about the grassroots momentum of the Bernie 2020 campaign. No one has figured out how to stop him. But Buttigieg is determined to do as much damage as he can.

Bernie's Pivot for Biden Isn't Pleasant. But Trump Must Be Defeated

April 16, 2020

THIS WEEK, SOON AFTER BERNIE SANDERS SUSPENDED HIS campaign, one of its most effective message-crafters summed up a vital challenge ahead, "The best hope to defeat Trump is to positively and constructively *motivate* a large Democratic turnout," David Sirota wrote. "The best way to do that is to show progressive voters they are actually valued, rather than taken for granted. And the best way to show them that they are valued is to actually embrace an agenda that they want."

Progressives should never stop fighting for policies that truly represent our values. And activists, unlike even the best politicians, can avoid the pitfalls of making diplomatic statements that aren't true.

While announcing the deactivation of his campaign on April 8, Bernie said that Joe Biden is "a very decent man." But decency is not a word that remotely applies to Biden's political record that spans several decades (as I've described in one article after another after another after another after another after another after another).

Ironically, at this historic juncture, Biden – a longtime eager corporate tool – is now the only electoral implement available to progressives for preventing the re-election of Trump. At this point, there's simply no other plausible way to prevent this monstrous president from winning a second term.

And so, in an interview with The Associated Press on Tuesday, Bernie spelled out a choice: "Do we be as active as we can in electing Joe Biden and doing everything we can to move Joe and his campaign in a more progressive direction? Or do we choose to sit it out and allow the most dangerous president in modern American history to get re-elected?"

Bernie started this week by endorsing Biden in an awkward video duet with the presumptive nominee. Symbolically, if not intentionally, when the video went to full screen while Bernie spoke, one object was clearly visible behind him – a chessboard.

There are reasons to criticize some of Bernie's recent tactical moves. (I wish he hadn't suspended his campaign before the end of primary voting.) But, looking ahead, he's being sensible about current political realities.

Crucially in swing states, Trump can only be defeated by votes for the Democratic presidential nominee, who's now virtually certain to be Biden, and there's no point in pretending otherwise. Magical thinking might be a wondrous literary device, but it's useless – or worse – in politics.

"We had a contentious campaign," Bernie told AP as he noted differences with Biden. "We disagree on issues. But my job now is to not only rally my supporters, but to do everything I can to bring the party together to see that [Trump] is not elected president."

(A bit paradoxically, Bernie said that he's hoping people will vote for him in the 20 or so states that have upcoming primaries – so that there'll be more Sanders delegates for the Democratic National Convention in August. More of those delegates will increase progressive leverage when the convention adopts a platform and sets future party rules.)

If anyone thinks it doesn't matter much whether Trump is re-elected, they're living in some kind of bubble. To those outside of such a soundproof bubble, Bernie is now sending an unequivocal message: "I believe that it's irresponsible for anybody to say, 'Well, I disagree with Joe Biden – I disagree with Joe Biden! – and therefore I'm not going to be involved.'"

Bernie Sanders is saying that progressives have a profound responsibility to fight against – and oust – the extreme right-wing forces that have gained control of the U.S. government's executive branch and, increasingly, the federal judiciary. Of course, in political terms, progressives wish that we were in a very different place. But this is where we are.

Corporate Democrats Are to Blame for Congressional Losses – So Naturally They're Blaming Progressives

November 15, 2020

CORPORATE DEMOCRATS GOT THE PRESIDENTIAL NOMINEE they wanted, along with control over huge campaign ad budgets and nationwide messaging to implement "moderate" strategies. But, as the *Washington Post* noted, Joe Biden's victory "came with no coattails down ballot." Democratic losses left just a razor-thin cushion in the House, and the party failed to win a Senate majority. Now, corporate Democrats are scapegoating progressives.

The best members of Congress are pushing back – none more forcefully or eloquently than Rashida Tlaib, the Michigan congresswoman who just won her second term in one of the nation's poorest districts. She was the most outspoken against an anti-progressive pile-on during a November 5 conference call of House Democrats. And she continues to hold high a shining lantern of progressive principles.

Tlaib has pointed out that "Democratic candidates in swing districts who openly supported progressive policies, like Medicare for All and the Green New Deal, won their races." And she refuses to retreat.

"We're not going to be successful if we're silencing districts like mine," she told *Politico* days ago. "Me not being able to speak on behalf of many of my neighbors right now, many of which are black neighbors, means me being silenced. I can't be silent."

Politico reported Tlaib was "choking up as she expressed frustration" near the end of an interview as she said: "If [voters] can walk past blighted homes and school closures and pollution to vote for Biden-Harris, when they feel like they don't have anything else, they deserve to be heard. I can't believe that people are asking them to be quiet."

In an email to supporters, Tlaib was clear: "We've got to focus on working class people. We are done waiting to be heard or prioritized by the federal government. I won't let leaders of either party silence my residents' voices any longer." Tlaib offers the kind of clarity that should guide progressive forces no matter how much "party unity" smoke is blown in their direction: "We are not interested in unity that asks people to sacrifice their freedom and their rights any longer. And if we truly want to unify our country, we have to really respect every single voice. We say that so willingly when we talk about Trump supporters, but we don't say that willingly for my black and brown neighbors and from LGBTQ neighbors or marginalized people."

When Rashida Tlaib talks about "pushing the Democratic Party to represent the communities that elected them," she actually means what she says. That's quite a contrast with the usual discourse coming from dominant Democrats and outfits like the Democratic National Committee. Let's face it: Most of the nearly 100 members of the Congressional Progressive Caucus are not reliable when corporate push comes to shove, assisted by House Speaker Nancy Pelosi. What has been startling and sometimes disturbing to entrenched Democrats is that Tlaib – along with House colleagues Alexandria Ocasio-Cortez, Ilhan Omar, Ro Khanna and some others – repeatedly make it clear that they're part of progressive movements. And those movements are serious about fundamental social change, even if it means polarizing with Democratic Party leaders.

Anyone with a shred of humane values should be aware that Republican lawmakers are anathema to those values. But that reality shouldn't blind us to the necessity of challenging – and, when feasible, organizing to unseat – elected Democrats who are more interested in maintaining the status quo that benefits moneyed interests than fighting for social justice.

While satisfying their impulses to blame the left for centrist failures, corporate Democrats and their mildly "progressive" enablers – inside and outside of Congress – are striving to paper over basic fault lines. The absence of a functional public-health system, the feeble government response to the climate emergency, the widening and deadly realities of income inequality, the systemic racism, the runaway militarism and so many other ongoing catastrophes are results of social structures that constrict democracy and serve oligarchy. Those who denounce the fight for a progressive agenda are telling us that, in essence, they don't want much to change.

From the desk of Pete Buttigieg (corrected)

December 19, 2020

BEING A CAREFUL PROOFREADER, I PROVIDED SOME VOLUNTEER assistance to Mayor Pete:

----- Forwarded message -----

From: Pete Buttigieg < info@wintheera.com >

Date: Wed, Dec 16, 2020

Subject: Thank you

From the desk of PETE BUTTIGIEG

Hi there,

Earlier today I stood on stage with President-elect Biden, where I was ~~humbled to be~~ paid off by being nominated to serve our nation as Secretary of Transportation.

Of course, as I look forward to taking on this new challenge and serving some of my most devoted paymasters on Wall Street, I can't help but reflect for a moment on the road we've traveled together to block the big, bad socialist, Bernie Sanders – and to feel a deep sense of gratitude for this community of supporters and especially for the corporate elites who made my presidential campaign so strong.

Whether you joined back when we were four people working out of a tiny office in downtown South Bend or signed up last week – to everyone who has been a part of this effort, talking to your family and friends, posting on social media, or chipping in when you could – I want to say thank you for ignoring my corkscrew double talk about healthcare and my overall misuse of my prodigious intellect to pander in highly circuitous ways.

Through it all, we've stuck to our Rules of the Road, well aware that the path to Pennsylvania Avenue power requires sucking up to corporate power – and Chasten and I are so grateful for the kindness you've shown to us at each step. You've proven that a politics built around who we can call to our side, where everyone can find belonging, isn't just possible – it's here. My solidarity with Amy and Beto to support Joe at the crucial moment is paying huge dividends.

Below are my remarks from today's event. And I wanted you to know I'm looking forward to when our paths will cross again when I try once again to bamboozle the public into believing I'm highly principled as I seek higher office and to seeing all the ways I know you will stay involved to help win the era to come – and to generate ever more creative propaganda from the "center" that has gotten us into calamitous situations that now afflict so many people in our nation.

Best,

Pete

Why Progressives Must Not Give Joe Biden a Political Honeymoon

December 20, 2020

THE THIRD TIME WOULD NOT BE A CHARM.

People on the left did very little to challenge Bill Clinton after he won the presidency in 1992. Two years later, a big Republican wave took control of Congress.

People on the left did very little to challenge Barack Obama after he won the presidency in 2008. Two years later, a big Republican wave took control of Congress.

Now, we're being told that people on the left should pipe down and do little to challenge Joe Biden. But silence or merely faint dissent would enable the third Democratic president in four decades to again sacrifice progressive possibilities on the altar of corporate power.

Clinton and Obama – no less than Biden in recent months – could sound like a semi-populist at times on the campaign trail. But during 16 years combined in the White House, they shared a governing allegiance to neoliberalism: aiding and abetting privatization, austerity budgets for the public sector, bloated budgets for the Pentagon, deregulation of corporate behavior, and so-called "free trade" agreements boosting big-business profit margins at the expense of workers, consumers and the environment.

The idea that corporate centrism is the best way for Democrats to defeat Republicans is belied by actual history. Yes, Clinton and Obama won re-election – but their political narcissism and fidelity to big corporations proved devastating to the Democratic Party and very helpful to the GOP.

During Obama's eight years as president, Democrats lost not only both houses of Congress but also more than 1,000 seats in state legislatures. As the *New York Times* noted, "In 2009, Democrats controlled both the state senate and house in 27 states, the Republicans 14. After the 2016 elections, Republicans controlled both branches of the legislatures in 32 states to 14 for the Democrats." Republicans also gained more governors.

It's worth pondering Obama's blunt assessment of his administration's first term: "My policies are so mainstream that if I had set the same policies that I had back in the 1980s, I would be considered a moderate Republican."

Yet the Obama era is now being fondly and routinely hailed as a kind of aspirational benchmark. We're now being told to yearn to go back to the future under the leadership of the soon-to-be president who boasted last year: "I'm an Obama-Biden Democrat, man, and I'm proud of it."

On the verge of 2021, populist anger and despair are unabated. And, as economic disasters worsen at macro and individual levels, more widespread populist rage is predictable. Only progressive populism offers an appealing alternative to the toxic pseudo-populism of the Trumpist Republican Party.

Pushing the Biden presidency in the direction of progressive populism is not only the morally correct thing to do, given the scale of human suffering and the existential threats posed by economic unraveling, the climate emergency and militarism. Progressive populism can also be the political antidote to the poisonous right-wing manipulation of genuine economic and social distress. In sharp contrast, "moderate" programs have little to offer.

My colleague Jeff Cohen describes the "No Honeymoon" campaign we're immersed in at RootsAction.org as "an effort to help save Biden from himself and from following in the footsteps – missteps, really – of his predecessors Obama and Clinton. Too much hesitation, vacillation, corporatism in the first two years will likely bring on a Republican landslide for Congress in 2022, as Clinton's vacillation and corporatism, like NAFTA, did in 1994, and Obama's in 2010, for example his bailing out Wall Street but not homeowners through a foreclosure freeze."

To avert a big Republican win in two years, Cohen says, "Biden has to deliver for poor, working-class and middle-class people. Policies that make a big difference in people's lives – including cancellation of federal student debt and pushing for a $15 federal minimum wage. That will mean listening more to progressive allies, progressive economists and legal experts – and less to the Democratic corporate donor class. If he doesn't deliver, Biden plays into the hands of the GOP faux-populists, setting us all up for defeat in 2022."

In the #NoHoneymoon launch video, released last week, former Bernie Sanders 2020 campaign national co-chair Nina Turner – now running for Congress in a special election – explained the concept of No Honeymoon. "We mean that we the people hold the power," she said. "That we must continue to fight for what is just, right and good, and fight against what is not just, right and good. We mean that we must have solidarity and commitment, one to another."

She added: "As long as there are injustices, we will continue to fight. What do we mean by that? We know that when everyday people put a little extra on the ordinary, extraordinary things happen.... We mean that we will not be seduced by smiles – we need action, and we need it right now. We will not relent. And that's what we mean when we say 'No Honeymoon.'"

Over the weekend, under the headline "Biden Cabinet Leans Centrist, Leaving Some Liberals Frustrated," the *New York Times* declared with typical media framing that "the president-elect's personnel choices are more pragmatic and familiar than ideological" – as though centrism itself is not "ideological." The newspaper reported that "there is no one yet in Mr. Biden's cabinet carrying the torch for the policies that he campaigned against during the primaries: free college for everyone, a costly Green New Deal, an anti-Wall Street agenda, universal health-care and steep increases in the minimum wage."

Silence or grumbling acquiescence as the Biden presidency takes shape would amount to a political repetition disorder of the sort that ushered in disastrous political results under the Clinton and Obama administrations. Progressives must now take responsibility and take action. As Nina Turner says, "everything we love is on the line."

2021

Joe Biden was hardly the first president to take office at a time of swiftly widening income inequality, but more than most he began to do something about it. His first year included backing and signing legislation with real benefits for tens of millions of Americans. Yet his resolve dissipated. Before the end of the year, Biden abandoned Build Back Better legislation that would have been transformational.

Notably, Biden withdrew all U.S. troops from Afghanistan in the late summer of 2021. But other approaches to foreign policy turned out to be problematic and worse. For instance, he refused to restore the better relations with Cuba that President Obama had achieved and Trump had destroyed, leaving cruel sanctions in place against that country and several others. Likewise, the Obama administration's great feat of the Iran nuclear deal, subsequently killed by Trump, was never to be revived by Biden.

Meanwhile, Biden went full speed ahead with plans for "modernization" of nuclear weapons that already had a price tag of $1.7 trillion. And he never wavered from support for ever-higher Pentagon spending – instead of devoting adequate resources to meeting human needs and protecting nature.

THE S.S. UNITED STATES

Denouncing Republican Evils Can't Do Much for the Biden Presidency Without Demanding Progressive Policies

January 11, 2021

THE REPUBLICAN PLUNGE INTO TRUMPISM HAS MADE THE party especially unhinged and dangerous, but its basic ideology has long been a shameless assault on minimal standards of human decency. Now – while Democratic leaders and most corporate media outlets are suitably condemning the fascist tendencies of Trump and his followers – deeper analysis and stepped-up progressive organizing are urgently needed.

Economic injustice – disproportionately harming people of color – constantly propels U.S. society in a downward spiral. Poverty, economic insecurity and political disempowerment go together. Systemic racism continues to thrive, enmeshed with the predatory routines of corporate power.

After becoming a member of Congress last week, Cori Bush wrote in the *Washington Post:* "Many have said that what transpired on Wednesday was not America. They are wrong. This is the America that Black people know. To declare that this is not America is to deny the reality that Republican members of the U.S. House and Senate incited this coup by treasonously working to overturn the results of the presidential election."

And, Bush added, "what my Republican colleagues call 'fraud' actually refers to the valid votes of Black, brown and Indigenous voters across this country who, in the midst of a pandemic that disproportionately kills us, overcame voter suppression in all of its forms to deliver an election victory for Joe Biden and Kamala D. Harris."

Yet that election victory – which was a huge blow to right-wing forces and a triumph for the progressive forces that made it possible – assures us of little. The same establishment-oriented corporate and militaristic mindsets that reigned supreme in the executive branch during the

Obama administration are being reconfigured for the Biden adminis-tration. Similar mentalities at the top of the Democratic Party a decade ago are replicated today.

But, at the grassroots, progressive outlooks are much more prevalent than a decade ago – and left-leaning forces are much better positioned. There's far less naiveté about Joe Biden on the verge of his presidency than there was a dozen years ago on the verge of Barack Obama's. And much stronger communication and organizing capacities are in place for progressive individuals and groups in 2021 than was true in 2009.

In short, as Biden prepares to move into the White House, progres-sives are in much better shape to put up a fight – not only against the right wing but also against corporate Democratic elites, who are uninterested in delivering the kind of broad-based economic uplift that could undermine the pseudo-populist propaganda coming from the Republican Party.

A day after the orchestrated mob assault at the Capitol, Bernie Sanders appeared on CNN and provided a cogent summary of what must be done to effectively push back against the Republicans. In contrast to standard-issue Democratic Party talking points, what he had to say went to the core of key economic and political realities.

While countless Democratic politicians and pundits were taking the easy route of only condemning Trump and his acolytes, Sanders went far deeper.

"We must not lose sight of the unprecedented pain and desperation felt by working people across the country as the pandemic surges and the economy declines," Sanders wrote to supporters on Sunday. "We must, immediately, address those needs."

Sanders pointed out that "right now, hunger is at the highest levels in decades in this country and the family that couldn't afford to put food on the table last week still cannot afford to put food on the table this week, and they need our help." Among the ongoing realities he cited were these:

> • "The 500,000 Americans who were homeless and the 30 million more facing eviction last week are still worried about keeping a roof over their heads this week, and they need our help."

- "During the midst of a murderous pandemic which is getting worse and worse every day, the 90 million Americans who were uninsured or underinsured last week still are worried about being able to afford to go to a doctor this week, and they need our help."

- "The millions of Americans working two or three jobs to pay the bills because we have a national minimum wage of $7.25 an hour this week will still be getting paid a starvation wage next week, and they need our help."

Such help will not come from merely denouncing the villainy of Trump and other Republicans. And it won't come from reflexively deferring to the Biden administration. On the contrary, it can come from insisting that there must be no honeymoon for the incoming administration if we want to meet the crying needs of working-class people.

Some progressives believe that we should give Biden a break as his presidency gets underway. But in early 1993, we were told to give President Clinton a break. Wall Streeters went into the Cabinet, NAFTA soon followed – and, in 1994, Republicans roared back and took Congress. Later came cruel "welfare reform," deregulation of the banking industry, and much more.

In early 2009, we were told to give a break to President Obama. Wall Streeters went into the Cabinet, big banks were bailed out while people with their houses under water lost their homes – and, in 2010, Republicans roared back and took Congress. Later came economic policies that undermined support and turnout from the Democratic Party base, helping Trump win four years ago.

As Bernie Sanders says, "The old way of thinking is what brought us Donald Trump."

The Sanders prescriptions for antidotes to right-wing poisons are absolutely correct. Along with ending Trump's toxic political career, Sanders wrote four days after the Capitol events, "we must also start passing an aggressive agenda that speaks to the needs of the working class in this country: income and wealth inequality, healthcare, climate change, education, racial justice, immigration and so many other vitally important issues. We must lift people out of poverty, revitalize American democracy, end the collapse of the middle class, and make certain our children and grandchildren are able to enjoy a quality of life that brings them health, prosperity, security and joy."

Sound impossible? It isn't. But to make such a future possible will require not only crushing the Republican Party but also dislodging the current Democratic Party leadership to make way for truly progressive elected Democrats – like Cori Bush, Rashida Tlaib, Ilhan Omar, Alexandria Ocasio Cortez, Ro Khanna and others – who understand that they must be part of transformative social movements that are our only hope.

Don't Let President Biden 'Make Us the Dupes of Our Hopes'

January 18, 2021

AT INAUGURATION TIME, JOURNALIST I. F. STONE WROTE, incoming presidents "make us the dupes of our hopes." That insight is worth pondering as Joe Biden ascends to the presidency. After four years of the real-life Trump nightmare, hope is overdue – but it's hazardous.

Stone astutely warned against taking heart from the lofty words that President Richard Nixon had just deployed in his inaugural address on January 20, 1969. With the Vietnam War raging, Stone pointed out: "It's easier to make war when you talk peace."

That's true of military war. And class war.

In 2021, class war is the elephant – and the donkey – in the national living room. Rhetoric aside, present-day Republican politicians are shameless warriors for wealthy privilege and undemocratic power that afflicts the non-rich. Democratic Party leaders aren't nearly as bad, but that's an extremely low bar; relatively few are truly champions of the working class, while most routinely run interference for corporate America, Wall Street and the military-industrial complex.

Rarely illuminated with clarity by corporate media, class war rages 24/7/365 in the real world. Every day and night, countless people are suffering and dying. Needlessly. From lack of social equity. From the absence of economic justice. From the greed and elite prerogatives cemented into the structures of politics and a wide range of institutions. From oligarchy that has gotten so extreme that three people in the United States (Jeff Bezos, Bill Gates and Warren Buffett) now possess more wealth than the entire bottom half of the population.

Yes, there are some encouraging signs about where the Biden presidency is headed. The intertwined economic crisis and horrific pandemic – combined with growing grassroots progressive pressure on the Democratic Party – have already caused Biden to move leftward on a range of crucial matters. The climate emergency and festering racial injustice also require responses. We can expect important steps via presidential executive orders before the end of this month.

At the same time, if past behavior is the best predictor of future behavior, we should not expect Biden to be a deserter from the class war that he has helped to wage, from the top down, throughout his political career – including via NAFTA, welfare "reform," the bankruptcy bill and financial-sector deregulation.

How far Biden can be pushed in better directions will depend on how well progressives and others who want humanistic change can organize. In effect, most of mass media will encourage us merely to hope – plaintively and passively – holding onto the sort of optimism that has long been silly putty in the hands of presidents and their strategists.

Hope is a human need, and recent Democratic presidents have been whizzes at catering to it. Bill Clinton marketed himself as "the man from Hope" (the name of his first hometown). Barack Obama authored the bestseller "The Audacity of Hope" that appeared two years before he won the White House. But projecting our hopes onto carefully scripted Rorschach oratory, on Inauguration Day or any day, is usually a surrender to images over realities.

The standard Democratic Party storyline is now telling us that greatness will be in reach for the Biden administration if only Republican obstacles can be overcome. Yet what has led to so much upheaval in recent years is mostly grounded in class war. And the positive aspects of Biden's initiatives should not delude progressives into assuming that Biden is some kind of a class-war ally. For the most part, he has been the opposite.

"Progressives are not going to get anything from the new administration unless they are willing to publicly pressure the new administration," David Sirota and Andrew Perez wrote days ago. "That means progressive lawmakers are going to have to be willing to fight and it means progressive advocacy groups in Washington are going to have to be willing to prioritize results rather than White House access."

The kind of access that progressives need most of all is access to our own capacities to realistically organize and gain power. It's a constant need – hidden in plain sight, all too often camouflaged by easier hopes.

More than being a time of hope – or fatalism – the inauguration of

President Joe Biden should be a time of skeptical realism and determination.

The best way to not become disillusioned is to not have illusions in the first place. And the best way to win economic and social justice is to keep organizing and keep pushing. What can happen during the Biden presidency is up for grabs.

Congresswoman Jayapal Misses the Mark by Saying Biden Deserves an 'A' Grade

May 9, 2021

IT'S THE JOB OF PROGRESSIVE ADVOCATES AND ACTIVISTS TO tell inconvenient truths, without sugarcoating or cheerleading. To effectively confront the enormous problems facing our country and world, progressives need to soberly assess everything – good, bad and mixed.

Yet last week, the chair of the Congressional Progressive Caucus, Pramila Jayapal, made headlines when she graded President Biden's job performance. "I give him an 'A' so far," Jayapal said in an otherwise well-grounded interview with the *Washington Post*. She conferred the top grade on Biden even though, as she noted, "that doesn't mean that I agree with him on every single thing."

Overall, the policies of the Biden administration have not come close to being consistently outstanding. Awarding an "A" to Biden is flatly unwarranted.

It's also strategically wrongheaded. If we're going to get maximum reforms in this crucial period, President Biden needs focused pressure – not the highest rating – from progressives. In school, an "A" grade commonly means "excellent performance" or "outstanding achievement." Rendering such a verdict on Biden's presidency so far promotes a huge misconception and lowers the progressive bar.

Biden does deserve credit for some strong high-level appointments (Deb Haaland as Interior Secretary jumps to mind), a number of important executive orders (many simply undoing four years of horrific Trumpism), and one crucial legislative achievement – the American Rescue Act. The proposed American Jobs Act (a small step toward a Green New Deal) and American Families Act (education/anti-poverty) are also quite progressive.

But Biden has made several major appointments that overtly kowtowed to corporate America – for example, "Mr. Monsanto" Tom Vilsack as Secretary of Agriculture and former venture capitalist Gina

Raimondo as Commerce Secretary. To mark Biden's first 100 days, the Revolving Door Project issued an overall grade of B- in its report card on how Biden had done in preventing "corporate capture" of the executive branch by industries such as fossil fuels, Big Pharma and Big Tech.

In an improvement over the Obama era, the Biden administration earned a B/B+ in keeping Wall Streeters from dominating its economic and financial teams. On the other hand, as graded by the Revolving Door Project, Biden got a D- on limiting the power of the military-industrial complex over U.S. foreign policy: "We are particularly alarmed by Biden's hiring of several alumni of the Center for a New American Security, a hawkish think tank funded by weapons manufacturers like Lockheed Martin and Northrop Grumman."

Much as "personnel is policy" in the executive branch, the federal budget indicates actual priorities. Biden's budget reflects his continuing embrace of the military-industrial complex, a tight grip that squeezes many billions needed for vital social, economic and environmental programs. The administration recently disclosed its plan to increase the basic military budget to $753 billion, a $13 billion boost above the last bloated Trump budget. (All told, the annual total of U.S. military-related spending has been way above $1 trillion for years.) And Biden continues to ramp up spending for nuclear weapons, including ICBMs – which former Defense Secretary William Perry aptly says are "some of the most dangerous weapons in the world."

Meanwhile, Biden is heightening the dangers of an unimaginably catastrophic war with Russia or China. In sharp contrast to his assertion on February 4 that "diplomacy is back at the center of our foreign policy," Biden proceeded to undermine diplomacy with reckless rhetoric toward Russia and a confrontational approach to China. The effects have included blocking diplomatic channels and signaling military brinkmanship.

Biden won praise when he announced plans for a not-quite-total U.S. troop withdrawal from Afghanistan, but he has not committed to ending the U.S. air war there – and some forms of on-the-ground military involvement are open-ended.

Unfortunately, little attention has gone to the alarming realities of Biden's foreign policy and inflated budget for militarism. Domestic matters are in the spotlight, where – contrary to overblown praise – the overall picture is very mixed.

While Biden has issued some executive orders improving social and regulatory policies, he has refused to issue many much-needed executive orders. Give him an "I" for incomplete, including on the issue of $1.7 trillion in student loan debt that undermines the economy and burdens 45 million debtors, especially people of color. Biden has not budged, even after non-progressive Democrats like Senate Majority Leader Chuck Schumer have pressed him to use his executive authority under existing legislation to excuse up to $50,000 in college debt per person.

On the subject of healthcare reform, Biden has long been held back by his allegiance to corporate power – as Representative Jayapal knows well, since she has tenaciously led the Medicare for All battle in the House. Biden has never disavowed his appalling comment in March 2020 that he might veto Medicare for All if it somehow passed both houses of Congress. During the traumatic 14 months of the pandemic since then, while millions have lost coverage because insurance is tied to employment, Biden's stance hardly improved. Candidate Biden had promised to lower the age of Medicare eligibility from 65 to 60, but even that meager promise has disappeared.

With wealth and income having gushed to the top in recent decades, and especially during Covid, Biden is proposing some tax increases on corporations and the very wealthy – quite popular with voters – to pay for infrastructure and social programs. For example, Biden proposes returning the top marginal tax bracket on the richest individuals from 37 percent to merely 39.6 percent, where it was in 2017 before Trump lowered it. Presidential candidate Bernie Sanders campaigned on raising the top tax bracket to 52 percent, while AOC called for raising it to 70 percent, a popular approach according to polls. To put this all in perspective: When the U.S. economy and middle class boomed during the 1950s, the top tax bracket was over 90 percent under Republican President Eisenhower.

There's no reason to quarrel with those who seek to inspire optimism among progressives by pointing out that their activism has already achieved some great things. But activism should be grounded in candor and realism about where we are now – and how far we still need to go.

Joe Biden's Relapse into Hallucinations About GOP Leaders

August 2, 2021

FOR A WHILE, PRESIDENT BIDEN SEEMED TO BE RECOVERING from chronic fantasies about Republicans in Congress. But last week he had a relapse – harming prospects for key progressive legislation and reducing the already slim hopes that the GOP can be prevented from winning control of the House and Senate in midterm elections 15 months from now.

Biden's reflex has been to gladhand his way across the aisle. On the campaign trail in May 2019, he proclaimed: "The thing that will fundamentally change things is with Donald Trump out of the White House. Not a joke. You will see an epiphany occur among many of my Republican friends." A year and a half later, the president-elect threw some bipartisan bromides into his victory speech – lamenting "the refusal of Democrats and Republicans to cooperate with one another," contending that the American people "want us to cooperate," and pledging "that's the choice I'll make."

But the notion of cooperating with Republican leaders like Senator Mitch McConnell and Representative Kevin McCarthy was always a fool's errand. That reality might as well have been blinking in big neon letters across the Capitol Dome since January, as Republicans continually doubled down on complete intransigence. By early March, when the landmark American Rescue Plan squeaked through Congress, Biden had new reasons to wise up.

Passage of the $1.9 trillion measure, Biden said, "proves we can do big things, important things in this country." But passage also proved that every Republican in the House and Senate is dedicated to stopping this country from doing "big, important things." The American Rescue Plan got through Congress without a single Republican vote.

As *The American Prospect*'s executive editor, David Dayen, pointed out at the time, many of the major gains in the rescue package were fundamental yet fragile. While purported "free-market solutions" had been set aside, crucial provisions were put on a timer to sunset: "We have the outline of a child allowance but it expires in a year. The [Affordable Care Act] subsidies expire in two years. The massive expansion of unemployment eligibility for a much wider group of workers is now done on Labor Day weekend. There's a modicum of ongoing public investment, but mostly this returns us to a steady state, with decisions to make from there."

Whether progress can be sustained and accelerated during the next several years will largely depend on ending Republican leverage over the Senate via the filibuster and preventing a GOP congressional majority from taking hold in January 2023. The new temporary measures, Dayen notes, could all be made permanent, "with automatic stabilizers that kick in during downturns, and Federal Reserve bank accounts for every American to fill when needed. We could ensure that federal support sustaining critical features of public life remains in place. We could choose to not build a pop-up safety net but an ongoing one."

The obstacles to enacting long-term structural changes will be heightened to the extent that Biden relapses into a futile quest for "bipartisanship." This year, the GOP's assaults on voting rights – well underway in numerous states controlled by Republican legislatures and governors – could be somewhat counteracted by strong, democracy-oriented federal legislation. And that won't happen if the Senate filibuster remains in place.

Yet Biden, even while denouncing attacks on voting rights, now seems quite willing to help Republicans retain the filibuster as a pivotal tool for protecting and enabling those attacks. During a CNN town hall last week, Biden said he favors tweaking the Senate rules to require that some senator keeps talking on the floor to continue a filibuster – but he's against getting rid of the filibuster. Eliminating it, Biden said, would "throw the entire Congress into chaos and nothing will get done." On voting rights, the president said, he wants to "bring along Republicans who I know know better."

Many activists quickly demolished those claims. "This answer from Biden on the filibuster just doesn't make sense," tweeted Sawyer Hackett, executive director of People First Future. "Republicans aren't going to wake up and 'know better' than suppressing the vote. The filibuster encourages them to obstruct and our reluctance to end it emboldens them to do worse."

The response from the president of the NAACP Legal Defense and Educational Fund, Sherrilyn Ifill, was aptly caustic: "What are their names? Name the Republicans who know better. This is not a strategy. The time for magical thinking is over."

As Biden slid into illogical ramblings on CNN to support retaining the filibuster, the implications were ominous and far-reaching. In the words of the Our Revolution organization, Biden "refused to support doing what must be done to secure voting rights. Despite all evidence to the contrary, he continues to entertain the possibility of getting 10 Republican votes for voting rights. Back here, in reality, precisely zero Republicans voted in support of the For the People Act, and there is no reason to expect that to change."

When Biden became president, the *Washington Post* reported that he had chosen to place a portrait of Franklin D. Roosevelt in the most prominent spot inside the Oval Office, as "a clear nod to a president who helped the country through significant crises, a challenge Biden now also faces." But Biden's recurrent yearning not to polarize with Republican leaders is in stark contrast to FDR's approach.

Near the end of his first term, in a Madison Square Garden speech condemning "the economic royalists," Roosevelt said: "They are unanimous in their hate for me – and I welcome their hatred." But now, in his recurrent search for cooperation, Biden seems eager for his Republican foes to like him. It's a ridiculous and dangerous quest.

Found in Translation: *New York Times* Says Democrats Shouldn't Challenge Oligarchy

November 10, 2021

A FEW DAYS AFTER THE NOVEMBER 2 ELECTION, THE *NEW York Times* published a vehement editorial calling for the Democratic Party to adopt "moderate" positions and avoid seeking "progressive policies at the expense of bipartisan ideas." It was a statement by the *Times* editorial board, which the newspaper describes as "a group of opinion journalists whose views are informed by expertise, research, debate and certain longstanding values."

The editorial certainly reflected "longstanding values" – since the *Times* has recycled them for decades in its relentless attacks on the progressive wing of the Democratic Party.

- The *Times* editorial board began its polemic by calling for the party to "return" to "moderate policies."

Translation: Stick to corporate-friendly policies of the sort that we applauded during 16 years of the Clinton and Obama presidencies.

- While scolding "a national Democratic Party that talks up progressive policies at the expense of bipartisan ideas," the editorial warned against "becoming a marginal Democratic Party appealing only to the left."

Translation: The Biden administration should reach across the aisle even more solicitously to the leadership of an obstructionist, largely racist, largely climate-change-denying, Trump-cultish Republican Party.

- The election results "are a sign that significant parts of the electorate are feeling leery of a sharp leftward push in the party, including on priorities like Build Back Better, which have some strong provisions and some discretionary ones driving up the price tag."

Translation: Although poll after poll shows that the Build Back Better agenda is popular with the broad public, especially increased

taxation on wealthy and corporate elites to pay for it, we need to characterize the plan as part of "a sharp leftward push."

> • "The concerns of more centrist Americans about a rush to spend taxpayer money, a rush to grow the government, should not be dismissed."

Translation: While we don't object to the ongoing "rush to spend taxpayer money" on the military, and we did not editorialize against the bloated Pentagon budget, we oppose efforts to "grow the government" too much for such purposes as healthcare, childcare, education, housing and mitigating the climate crisis.

> • "Mr. Biden did not win the Democratic primary because he promised a progressive revolution. There were plenty of other candidates doing that. He captured the nomination – and the presidency – because he promised an exhausted nation a return to sanity, decency and competence."

Translation: No need to fret about the anti-democratic power of great wealth and corporate monopolies. We liked the status quo before the Trump presidency, and that's more or less what we want now.

> • "'Nobody elected him to be FDR,' Representative Abigail Spanberger, a moderate Democrat from Virginia, told the *Times* after Tuesday's drubbing."

Translation: Spanberger, a former CIA case officer and current member of the corporate Blue Dog Coalition in Congress, is our kind of Democrat.

> • "Democrats should work to implement policies to help the American people."

Translation: Democrats should work to implement policies to help the American people but not go overboard by helping them too much. We sometimes write editorials bemoaning the vast income inequality in this country, but we don't want the government to do much to reduce it.

> • "Congress should focus on what is possible, not what would be possible if Joe Manchin, Kyrsten Sinema and – frankly – a host of lesser-known Democratic moderates who haven't had to vote on policies they might oppose were not in office."

Translation: We editorialize about social justice, but we don't want structural changes and substantial new government policies that could bring it much closer. We editorialize about the climate crisis, but not in favor of government actions anywhere near commensurate with the crisis. Our type of tepid liberalism is an approach that won't be a bottom-line threat to the *Times* owners and big advertisers – and won't diminish the leverage and holdings of wealthy elites, including the New York Times Company's chairman A.G. Sulzberger and the company's board of directors. We want change, but not too much!

- "Democrats agree about far more than they disagree about. But it doesn't look that way to voters after months and months of intraparty squabbling. Time to focus on – and pass – policies with broad support."

Translation: Although progressives are fighting for programs that actually do have broad public support, we'll keep declaring those programs don't have broad public support. Progressives should give up and surrender to the corporate forces we like to call "moderate."

2022

During his second year in the Oval Office, Joe Biden lapsed into his more customary "moderate" political mode, while his capacity to speak coherently weakened. Party discipline, internalized by Democrats in Congress, precluded much independent-minded leadership from them. Obedience to President Biden was the Democratic norm.

Biden hype got a boost from the midterm elections. His boosters stoked claims that the results showed Biden's electoral clout and impressive fitness to run for a second term. But – as a Democratic member of Congress anonymously told the *New York Times* – the reality was the opposite. Biden's unpopularity with voters had been harmful to Democratic candidates.

Despite their private concerns, Democrats in Congress began to fall all over themselves declaring that Biden should run for re-election. Conformity of groupthink and fear of retribution from the White House kept people quiet when they should have spoken up and might have altered the course of history for the better.

WHAT DOESN'T KILL
YOU MUTATES
AND TRIES AGAIN
TRUMP
TRUMP
OATH
KEEPERS
STOP
THE
STEAL
M.WUERKER
POLITICO
Andrews McMeel

Grassroots Organizing Should Dump Biden and Clear the Path for a Better Nominee in 2024

July 13, 2022

PUNDITS ARE FOCUSED ON JOE BIDEN'S TANKING POLL numbers, while progressives continue to be alarmed by his dismal job performance. Under the apt headline "President Biden Is Not Cutting the Mustard," last week *The American Prospect* summed up: "Young people are abandoning him in droves because he won't fight for their rights and freedom." Ryan Cooper wrote that "at a time when Democrats are desperate for leadership – especially some kind of strategy to deal with a lawless and extreme Supreme Court – he is missing in action."

Yes, Senators Joe Manchin and Kyrsten Sinema team up with Republicans to stymie vital measures. But the president's refusal to issue executive orders that could enact such popular measures as canceling student debt and many other policies has been part of a derelict approach as national crises deepen. Recent events have dramatized the downward Biden spiral.

Biden's slow and anemic response to the Supreme Court's long-expected Dobbs decision overturning Roe v. Wade spotlighted the magnitude of the stakes and the failure. The grim outlook has been underscored by arrogance toward progressive activists. Consider this statement from White House communications director Kate Bedingfield last weekend as she reacted to wide criticism: "Joe Biden's goal in responding to Dobbs is not to satisfy some activists who have been consistently out of step with the mainstream of the Democratic Party. It's to deliver help to women who are in danger and assemble a broad-based coalition to defend a woman's right to choose now, just as he assembled such a coalition to win during the 2020 campaign."

The traditional response to such arrogance from the White House toward the incumbent's party base is to grin – or, more likely, grimace – and bear it. But that's a serious error for concerned individuals and organizations. Serving as enablers to bad policies and bad politics is hardly wise.

Polling released by the *New York Times* on Monday highlighted that most of Biden's own party doesn't want him to run for re-election, "with 64 percent of Democratic voters saying they would prefer a new standard-bearer in the 2024 presidential campaign." And "only 26 percent of Democratic voters said the party should renominate him."

A former ambassador to Portugal who was appointed by President Obama, Allan Katz, has made a strong case for Biden to announce now that he won't run for re-election. Writing for *Newsweek* under the headline "President Biden: I'm Begging You – Don't Run in 2024. Our Country Needs You to Stand Down," Katz contended that such an announcement from Biden would remove an albatross from the necks of Democrats facing tough elections in the midterms.

In short, to defeat as many Republicans as possible this fall, Biden should be seen as a one-term president who will not seek the Democratic nomination in 2024.

Why push forward with this goal? The #DontRunJoe campaign that our team at RootsAction launched this week offers this explanation: "We felt impelled to intervene at this time because while there is a mainstream media debate raging over whether Joe Biden should run again, that discussion is too narrow and lacking in substance – focused largely on his age or latest poll numbers. We object to Biden running in 2024 because of his job performance as president. He has proven incapable of effectively leading for policies so badly needed by working people and the planet, including policies he promised as a candidate."

It's no secret that Republicans are very likely to win the House this November, probably by a large margin. And the neofascist GOP has a good chance of winning the Senate as well, although that could be very close. Defeating Republicans will be hindered to the extent that progressive and liberal forces circle the political wagons around an unpopular president in a defense of the unacceptable status quo.

While voters must be encouraged to support Democrats – the only way to beat Republicans – in key congressional races this fall, that should not mean signing onto a quest to renew Biden's lease on the White House. RootsAction has emphasized: "While we are announcing the Don't Run Joe campaign now, we are urging progressive, anti-racist, feminist and pro-working-class activists to focus on defeating the right wing in this November's elections. Our all-out launch will come on November 9, 2022 – the day after those midterm elections."

With all the bad news and negative polling about Biden in recent weeks, the folly of touting him for a second term has come into sharp focus. While the president insists that he plans to run again, he has left himself an escape hatch by saying that will happen assuming he's in good health. But what we should do is insist that – whatever his personal health might be – the health of the country comes first. Democratic candidates this fall should not be hobbled by the pretense that they're asking voters to support a scenario of six more years for President Biden.

It's time to create a grassroots groundswell that can compel Joe Biden to give public notice – preferably soon – that he won't provide an assist to Republican forces by trying to extend his presidency for another four years. A pledge to voluntarily retire at the end of his first term would boost the Democratic Party's chances of getting a stronger and more progressive ticket in 2024 – and would convey in the meantime that Democratic candidates and the Biden presidency are not one and the same.

Biden Made It Harder for Democrats to Win. He'd Be an Albatross on the 2024 Ticket.

November 9, 2022

NO AMOUNT OF POST-ELECTION PUFFERY ABOUT JOE BIDEN CAN change a key political reality: His approval ratings are far below the public's positivity toward the Democratic Party. Overall, the Democrats who won the midterm elections did so despite Biden, not because of him. He's a drag on the party, a boon to Republicans, and – if he runs again – he'd be a weak candidate against the GOP nominee in the 2024 presidential campaign.

While the electorate is evenly split between the two parties, there's no such close division about Biden. NBC reported its exit poll on Tuesday "found that two-thirds of voters (68 percent) do not want Biden to run for president again in 2024."

This is nothing new. Biden's low public-approval ratings have been longstanding. A chart showing chronic disapproval now has him at a dozen points underwater – 53 percent "disapprove" and only 41 percent "approve." The gap between approval of Biden and of his party underscores what a leaden weight he is on Democratic electoral prospects.

As for how he's apt to govern next year, Biden has offered a willingness to compromise with the right-wing Republican leadership. A *New York Times* headline after his Wednesday afternoon news conference summed up: "Biden Promises Bipartisanship After a Red Wave 'Didn't Happen.'"

But "bipartisanship" is exactly what we don't need, in the face of extremist Republican demagogues who are determined to keep dragging the goal posts – and the country – further rightward.

In contrast to the current fad of adulation for Biden in much of corporate media, *Politico* offered this sober assessment of his impacts on the midterms: "It's hard to argue that Democrats over-performed on Tuesday because of Biden rather than in spite of him. His approval rating, hovering around 41 percent, is dismal – and has been all year. He'll turn 80 this month, and earlier this year, a majority of Democrats polled said they'd prefer someone else to be the party's nominee."

The article added: "But one thing Biden did have going for him was the calendar, and the reluctance of Democrats to do anything that might hurt him – and, by extension, the party – ahead of the midterms. That imperative is gone now. And though no prominent Democrat is likely to run a serious campaign against Biden, there will be increasing pressure on him, especially from the left, to step aside."

It will be crucial to boost that pressure in the months ahead, which is why I'm glad to be part of the Don't Run Joe organizing team. On Wednesday, the campaign launched digital ads reaching Democratic voters in New Hampshire with the message that "we need strong leadership to defeat Republicans in 2024." And, while beating the fascistic GOP will be absolutely necessary, moving ahead with vital progressive policies will also be of paramount importance.

In New Hampshire, which has long hosted the nation's first presidential primary, Democratic State Representative Sherry Frost said this on Wednesday:

> I am eager to support a candidate who understands the fatal dysfunction in our economy and is willing to hold the ultra-wealthy individuals and corporations to their obligations to the rest of us, who is going to actively champion meaningful civil rights and voting protections, and who will spearhead a shift away from the military-industrial complex and oligarchy and toward a culture that works for the most vulnerable of us first. I am not confident that Biden is that candidate, and while I appreciate his rescuing us from another Trump term, I believe we need someone else to champion the big and systemic changes we need to continue to strive toward our more perfect union.

What does all this mean for people who want to defeat Republicans in 2024 and to advance truly progressive agendas? Joe Biden should not be the Democratic Party's presidential nominee. If he runs for re-election – representing the status quo – the outcome would likely be disastrous. Grassroots activism will be essential to create better alternatives.

Biden Wants to Prevent a Strong Primary Challenge. He Shouldn't Get Away With It

December 5, 2022

JOE BIDEN HAS DIRECTED THE DEMOCRATIC NATIONAL Committee to reduce the danger that progressives might effectively challenge him in the 2024 presidential primaries. That's a key goal of his instructions to the DNC last week, when Biden insisted on dislodging New Hampshire – the longtime first-in-the-nation primary state where he received just 8 percent of the vote and finished fifth in the 2020 Democratic primary. No wonder Biden wants to replace New Hampshire with South Carolina, where he was the big primary winner.

The White House and mainstream journalists have echoed each other to assert that Biden would face no serious challenge to renomination if he runs again. But his blatant intrusion into the DNC's process for setting the primary calendar is a sign of anxiety about potential obstacles to winning renomination.

Unlike all other states under consideration for early primaries, South Carolina is not a battleground state. Everyone knows that the Democratic ticket won't come close to winning in deep-red South Carolina in 2024. But that state – which Biden obviously sees as vital to his renomination – has a party apparatus dominated by Biden's powerful corporatist ally, Congressman James Clyburn.

The Biden plan to reorder the 2024 schedule "includes a subtle but effective ploy to minimize the chances that he'd face a left-wing challenger in the primaries if the 80-year-old president, as expected, seeks a second term," centrist Walter Shapiro wrote approvingly in *The New Republic*. "More than that, Biden has created a template beyond 2024 to lessen the odds that future versions of Bernie Sanders will get liftoff in the early Democratic primaries."

But serious public discussion from candidates with a range of outlooks is badly needed in the process of selecting the presidential nominee. From healthcare, extreme economic inequality, labor rights and racial justice to military spending, foreign policy and the climate emergency, voters in Democratic primaries need to hear crucial issues debated.

The current prevailing attitudes are retrograde. While Democratic politicians and pundits weigh in on whether Joe Biden should run for president again, his party's voters are presumed to be little more than spectators. But the decision on whether Biden will be the nominee in 2024 shouldn't be his alone. A party that has been emphasizing the importance of democracy should not be so eager to short-circuit it in the presidential nominating process.

Very few congressional Democrats have been willing to publicly depart from the party line that Biden would be a fine standard-bearer. The few dissenting voices among them are usually furtive. The *New York Times* reported after the midterm election that a House Democrat – speaking "on the condition of anonymity to avoid antagonizing the White House" – said that "Biden's numbers were 'a huge drag' on Democratic candidates, who won in spite of the president not thanks to him."

Fears of antagonizing the White House have sealed Democratic office-holders inside a bubble that carries them away from the party's grass-roots base. This fall began with most Democratic voters not wanting Biden to be the party's nominee next time. Even amid post-midterms euphoria among Democrats, they are now evenly split on the question. But Democrats on Capitol Hill and other party leaders remain frozen in place, rarely casting any doubt on the wisdom of renominating this president.

The disconnect from the party's base is in sync with a refusal to acknowledge the facts indicating that Biden at the top of the ticket would be an albatross around the necks of Democratic candidates in 2024. While voters are evenly divided between the two major parties, Biden's public-approval deficit has exceeded 10 percent almost all of this year. Nine out of 10 young adults – a key cohort for Democratic prospects – don't want him to run for re-election. In midterm exit polling, two-thirds of voters said they didn't want Biden to run. Yet, when asked about those survey results, the president fell back on "watch me" bravado.

We're told that smoke-filled rooms are a thing of the past in national politics. But when a president wants to run for re-election, the anticipated mode is not much better. Looking ahead, the only way to inject participatory democracy into the Democrats' nominating process for 2024 is to insist that the nomination should be earned with the party's voters, not bestowed from on high.

If President Biden decides to seek the Democratic nomination, as now seems likely, credible primary challengers could enliven an otherwise stultifying process, making it robust instead of a bust. The corrosive effects of stagnated assumptions should be held up to disinfecting sunlight. New ideas should be discussed rather than suppressed.

Conventional wisdom insists that a president has the divine political right to be the party's nominee for a second term. But a president is not a party's king, and he has no automatic right to renomination.

2023

The real-life Shakespearean tragedy of President Biden unfolded as he threw down a gauntlet to run for re-election. With rare exceptions, elected Democrats fell in line and feigned enthusiasm even while often privately voicing trepidation. Meanwhile, Biden's mental frailty and cognitive decline became evermore evident.

Biden enablers at the top of the Democratic Party were distant from its base, as polling showed that most of the party's voters did not want him to be the next nominee. Skepticism dappled through news media, but a common canard – pushed by Biden's sycophants at the White House – contended that because he had defeated Trump once, he was the best person to do it again. The claim ignored the fact that Trump 2020 had represented an unpopular status quo, and Biden 2024 would represent an even more unpopular status quo, as "right track / wrong track" polling made crystal clear.

Soon after Hamas attacked Israel on October 7 and the Israeli military began its siege of Gaza, Biden moved into lockstep with Benjamin Netanyahu's government, boosting huge no-strings U.S. military aid as the slaughter of Palestinian civilians escalated.

HEY, THE 80s ARE THE NEW 79s!
Pollyanna & Assoc.
DEMOCRATIC STRATEGISTS
VOTE JOE
STICK WITH Biden
VOTE JOE 2024
Joltin' JOE
Hair
M.WUERKER
POLITICO
Andrews McMeel

Biden to Democrats: Nominate Me, Whether You Like It or Not

January 6, 2023

WITH 2023 UNDERWAY, DEMOCRATS IN OFFICE ARE STILL dodging the key fact that most of their party's voters don't want President Biden to run for re-election. Among prominent Democratic politicians, deference is routine while genuine enthusiasm is sparse. Many of the endorsements sound rote. Late last month, retiring senator Patrick Leahy of Vermont came up with this gem: "I want him to do whatever he wants. If he does, I'll support him."

Joe Biden keeps saying he intends to be the Democratic nominee in 2024. Whether he will be is an open question – and progressives should strive to answer it with a firm No. The next presidential election will be exceedingly grim if all the Democratic Party can offer as an alternative to the neofascist Republican Party is an incumbent who has so often served corporate power and consistently serves the military-industrial complex.

The Biden administration has taken some significant antitrust steps to limit rampant monopolization. But overall realities are continuing to widen vast economic inequalities that are grist for the spinning mill of pseudo-populist GOP demagogues. Meanwhile, President Biden rarely conveys a sense of urgency or fervent discontent with present-day social conditions. Instead, he routinely comes off as "status-quo Joe."

For the future well-being of so many millions of people, and for the electoral prospects of the Democratic Party in 2024, representing the status quo invites cascading disasters. A few months ago, Bernie Sanders summed up this way: "The most important economic and political issues facing this country are the extraordinary levels of income and wealth inequality, the rapidly growing concentration of ownership, the long-term decline of the American middle class and the evolution of this country into oligarchy."

Interviewed days ago, Sanders said: "It pains me very, very much that we're seeing more and more working-class people voting Republican. Politically, that is a disaster, and Democrats have to recognize that serious problem and address it."

But President Biden doesn't seem to recognize the serious problem, and he fails to address it.

During the last two years, domestic policy possibilities have been curbed by Biden's frequent and notable refusals to use the power of the presidency for progress. He did not issue many of the potential executive orders that could have moved the country forward despite Senate logjams. At the same time, "bully pulpit" advocacy for workers' rights, voter rights, economic justice, climate action and much more has been muted or nonexistent.

Biden seems unable or unwilling to articulate a social-justice approach to such issues. As for the continuing upward spike in Pentagon largesse while giving human needs short shrift, Biden was full of praise for the record-breaking, beyond-bloated $858 billion military spending bill that he signed in late December.

While corporate media's reporters and pundits are much more inclined to critique his age than his policies, what makes Biden most problematic for so many voters is his antiquated political approach. Running for a second term would inevitably cast Biden as a defender of current conditions – in an era when personifying current conditions is a heavy albatross that weighs against electoral success.

A Hart Research poll of registered voters in November found that only 21 percent said the country was "headed in the right direction" while 72 percent said it was "off on the wrong track." As the preeminent symbol of the way things are, Biden is all set to be a vulnerable standard-bearer in a country where nearly three-quarters of the electorate say they don't like the nation's current path.

But for now anyway, no progressive Democrat in Congress is willing to get into major trouble with the Biden White House by saying he shouldn't run, let alone by indicating a willingness to challenge him in the early 2024 primaries. Meanwhile, one recent poll after another showed that nearly 60 percent of Democrats don't want Biden to run again. A *New York Times* poll last summer found that a stunning 94 percent of Democrats under 30 years old would prefer a different nominee.

Although leaning favorably toward Biden overall, mass-media coverage has occasionally supplied the kind of candor that Democratic officeholders have refused to provide on the record. "The party's relief over holding the Senate and minimizing House losses in the midterms has gradually given way to collective angst about what it means if Biden runs again," NBC News reported days before Christmas.

Conformist support from elected Democrats for another Biden campaign reflects a shortage of authentic representation on Capitol Hill. The gap is gaping, for instance, between leaders of the Congressional Progressive Caucus and the constituency – the progressive base – they claim to represent. In late November, CPC chair Pramila Jayapal highlighted the gap when she went out of her way to proclaim that "I believe he should run for another term and finish this agenda we laid out."

Is such leadership representing progressives to the establishment or the other way around?

Biden Wielding DNC to Guard Against Progressive Challenge

January 30, 2023

WHEN THE DEMOCRATIC NATIONAL COMMITTEE CONVENES ITS winter meeting on Thursday in Philadelphia, a key agenda item will be rubber-stamping Joe Biden's manipulation of next year's presidential primaries. There'll be speeches galore, including one by Biden as a prelude to his expected announcement that he'll seek a second term. The gathering will exude confidence, at least in public. But if Biden were truly confident that Democratic voters want him to be the 2024 nominee, he wouldn't have intervened in the DNC's scheduling of early primaries.

New polling underscores why Biden is so eager to bump New Hampshire from the first-in-the-nation spot that it has held for more than 100 years. In the state, "two-thirds of likely Democratic primary voters don't want President Joe Biden to seek re-election," the UNH Survey Center found. "Biden is statistically tied with several 2020 rivals, including Transportation Secretary Pete Buttigieg, Massachusetts Senator Elizabeth Warren and Vermont Senator Bernie Sanders, all of whom are more personally popular than Biden among likely Democratic primary voters in New Hampshire."

Dismal as Biden's showing was in the new poll, it was a step up from his actual vote total in New Hampshire's 2020 primary, when he came in fifth with 8 percent of the vote. No wonder Biden doesn't want the state to go first and potentially set primary dominoes falling against him.

Keen to reduce the chances of a major primary challenge next year, Biden sent a letter to the DNC in early December insisting on a new schedule – demoting New Hampshire to a second spot, alongside Nevada, while giving the leadoff slot to South Carolina. Democratic Party energy and funds will be squandered in that deep-red state, which is about as likely to give its electoral votes to the 2024 Democratic ticket as Ron DeSantis is likely to donate the money in his campaign coffers to the Movement for Black Lives.

But South Carolina, the state with the lowest rate of unionization in the country, offers the singular virtue of having rescued Biden's presidential hopes with its 2020 primary. As The Associated Press explained last week, Biden is "seeking to reward South Carolina, where nearly 27 percent of the population is Black, after a decisive win there revived his 2020 presidential campaign following losses it suffered in Iowa, New Hampshire and Nevada."

The president's rationalization for putting South Carolina first is diversity. Yet the neighboring purple state of Georgia, which has an activist Democratic base, is more racially diverse – and it's a crucial swing state, where the party's general-election prospects would benefit from being the first-in-the-nation presidential primary.

Biden's intervention has created a long-term political mess for Democrats in New Hampshire, where he's now less popular than ever due to undermining the state's first-primary status. Even New Hampshire's normally compliant Democratic senators and representatives in Congress have been denouncing the move. Biden's maneuver has boosted the chances that the Democratic ticket will lose the state's four electoral votes this time around.

But Biden having his way with the Democratic National Committee is a slam dunk because he supplies the ball, hires the referees, owns the nets and controls the concession stands. While cowed DNC members dribble at his behest, substantial concerns will echo outside the range of officials' whistles.

As a Don't Run Joe full-page ad in *The Hill* newspaper pointed out last week (full disclosure: I helped write it), "There are ample indications that having Joe Biden at the top of ballots across the country in autumn 2024 would bring enormous political vulnerabilities for the ticket and for down-ballot races."

But so far, like the Democrats in Congress, members of the DNC have indicated much more concern about avoiding the ire of the Biden White House than avoiding the probable grim outcome of a Biden '24 campaign. By the time the DNC adjourns on Saturday, news reports will be filled with on-the-record statements from members lauding Biden's leadership with next year's elections on the horizon. Conformity prevails.

But warning signs are profuse. Among the latest are results of a

YouGov poll released days ago: "Just 34 percent of Americans describe Biden as honest and trustworthy – a new low for his presidency. That's an 8-point drop from when this question was last asked in December 2022, prior to the public revelation that classified documents had been found in Biden's possession."

This is the electoral horse that Democrats are supposed to be riding into battle against the extremist Republican Party next year. The national Democratic Party is locked into operating at the whim of a president now believed to be "honest and trustworthy" by only one-third of U.S. adults.

How all this will play out at the DNC meeting is hardly a mystery. Yet many members surely know that Biden is likely to be a weak candidate if he goes ahead with proclaimed plans to run for re-election. The hope is that the GOP will defeat itself as an extremist party in disarray. But it would be irresponsible to gamble on such a scenario by rolling dice loaded with Biden.

Elected Democrats Are Conformist Enablers of Biden for 2024

September 25, 2023

RECENT NEWS REPORTS HAVE BEEN FILLED WITH RESULTS of one poll after another after another showing that President Biden continues to weaken as a candidate for re-election. With an overall approval rating now 21 points underwater, polling shows he has lost support among key demographics that made his 2020 victory possible – especially the young and people of color. Alarm bells among pro-Biden pundits have finally begun to break the political sound barrier.

But on Capitol Hill, all's quiet on the Democratic front.

A gap has grown vast between current assessments from media, largely based on voter opinion data, and current public claims from congressional Democrats who keep their nose to the talking-points grindstone. An effect is that party leaders and backbenchers alike are losing credibility with the party's base.

The gap is so lopsided that a poll this month found 67 percent of "Democrats and Democratic-leaning independent voters" said they don't want Biden to run again. Meanwhile, no more than 1 percent of Democrats in Congress are willing to say so in public. By any measure, a disconnect between 67 and 1 percent is, uh, substantial.

For Democratic lawmakers to be so untethered from the people who elected them tells you a lot about the compliant relationship that usually prevails among elected Democrats toward President Biden. And it signifies an unhealthy relationship between Democrats in office and the party's activist base.

While supposedly representing a progressive grassroots base to the political establishment, some members of Congress end up routinely representing the political establishment to the progressive grassroots base.

The dire need for progressive advances in government policies is undermined when elected Democrats reflexively echo the Biden 2024 campaign line and pretend that he's a sufficiently strong candidate to defeat the neofascist Republican Party next year. When deferring to congressional Democrats who in turn defer to the man in the Oval Office, progressive activists and organizations end up functioning more like supplicants than constituents in a representative democracy.

But hope springs eternal, and so does fear of angering the White House. With the start of presidential primaries just a few months away, the crux of the matter is that Democrats in Congress are opting for self-focused, risk-averse conformity rather than visionary leadership.

Now – while even pro-Biden media like CNN and MSNBC are, at last, sounding more realistic about Biden's severe electoral deficits – prominent Democrats are either keeping quiet about the grim odds of a 2024 political train wreck or are spouting feel-good nonsense worthy of the myopic Mr. Magoo. The more that Democrats in the House and Senate declare how great Biden will be as the party's standard-bearer next year, the more it seems they've been swallowed up by a Capitol Hill bubble.

Yet mainstream media outlets are now underscoring the wide distance between the Democratic players on the Hill and the Democratic voters who've put them there. NBC News brought it all into focus, summing up: "When party elites look at President Joe Biden, they see the second coming of Franklin D. Roosevelt. When voters view the president, many see an old man."

More importantly, many hear timeworn ideas and promises that ring hollow. Working-class voters can see and hear a president who has refused to really fight for their economic interests, while corporate greed has been raising prices. It's an invitation to eye-rolling from core Democratic constituencies when Biden and his advocates proclaim how he's going to go all-out to fight for their interests in the second term after he hasn't done so in the first.

To Democratic officeholders, worried about retaining the presidency and their own seats, such matters might seem relatively unimportant. But bleak electoral consequences are foreseeable. Biden has declined to use the bully pulpit to battle for progressive measures that are poll-tested and popular with the electorate.

Democrats in Congress have ample reasons to be apprehensive about next year. But their silences and spin increasingly make them look more like PR specialists than leaders. The more they prop up Joe Biden to run for re-election, the better Donald Trump likes the odds he'll return to the White House.

Biden Is a Genocide Denier and the "Enabler in Chief" for Israel's Ongoing War Crimes

October 29, 2023

FOR THREE WEEKS, PRESIDENT BIDEN HAS PLAYED A KEY ROLE in backing Israel's war crimes while touting himself as a compassionate advocate of restraint. That pretense is lethal nonsense as Israel persists with mass killing of civilians in Gaza.

The same crucial standards that fully condemned Hamas's murders of Israeli civilians on October 7 should apply to Israel's ongoing murders that have already taken the lives of at least several times as many Palestinian civilians. And Israel is just getting started.

"We need an immediate ceasefire," Congresswoman Rashida Tlaib wrote in an email Saturday evening, "but the White House and Congress continue to unconditionally support the Israeli government's genocidal actions."

That unconditional support makes Biden and the vast majority of Congress directly complicit with mass murder and genocide, defined as "the deliberate killing of a large number of people from a particular nation or ethnic group with the aim of destroying that nation or group." The definition clearly fits the words and deeds of Israel's leaders.

"Israel has dropped approximately 12,000 tons of explosives on Gaza so far and has reportedly killed multiple senior Hamas commanders, but the majority of the casualties have been women and children," *Time* magazine summed up at the end of last week. Israel's military has been shamelessly slaughtering civilians in homes, stores, markets, mosques, refugee camps and healthcare facilities. Imagine what can be expected now that communications between Gaza and the outside world are even less possible.

For reporters, being on the ground in Gaza is very dangerous; Israel's assault has already killed at least 29 journalists. For the Israeli government, the fewer journalists alive in Gaza the better; media reliance on Israeli handouts, news conferences and interviews is ideal.

Pro-Israel frames of reference and word choices are routine in U.S. mainstream media. Yet some exceptional reporting has shed light on the merciless cruelty of Israel's actions in Gaza, where 2.2 million people live.

For example, on October 28, "PBS News Weekend" provided a human reality check as Israel began a ground assault while stepping up its bombing of Gaza. "As Israeli ground operations intensified there, suddenly the phone and internet signal went out," correspondent Leila Molana-Allen reported. "So, people in Gaza, voiceless through the night as they were under these intense bombardments. People were unable to call ambulances, and we've heard this morning that ambulance drivers were standing at high points throughout, trying to see where the explosions were, so they could just drive directly there. People unable to communicate with their families to see if they're alright. People this morning saying 'we've been digging children out of the rubble with our bare hands because we can't call for help.'"

While people in Gaza "are under some of the most intense bombardment we've ever seen," Molana-Allen added, they have no safe place to go: "Even though they're still being told to move to the south, in fact most people can't get to the south because they have no fuel for their cars, they can't travel, and even in the south bombardment continues."

Meanwhile, Biden has continued to publicly express his unequivocal support for what Israel is doing. After he spoke with Israeli Prime Minister Benjamin Netanyahu last week, the White House issued a statement without the slightest mention of concern about what Israel's bombing was inflicting on civilians. Instead, the statement said, "the President reiterated that Israel has every right and responsibility to defend its citizens from terrorism and to do so in a manner consistent with international humanitarian law."

Biden's support for continuing the carnage in Gaza is matched by Congress. As Israel began its fourth week of terrorizing and killing, only 18 members of the House were on the list of lawmakers cosponsoring H.Res. 786, "Calling for an immediate de-escalation and ceasefire in Israel and occupied Palestine." All of those 18 cosponsors are people of color.

While Israel kills large numbers of Palestinian civilians each day – and clearly intends to kill many thousands more – we can see "progressive" masks falling away from numerous members of Congress who remain cravenly frozen in political conformity.

"In a dark time," poet Theodore Roethke wrote, "the eye begins to see."

Backing Biden for 2024, Conformist Democrats Have Been in Denial. Now They're in a Panic

November 26, 2023

OVER THE WEEKEND, *POLITICO* PUBLISHED THE LATEST IN A tidal wave of stories about President Biden's dwindling prospects for re-election. Under the headline "The Polls Keep Getting Worse for Biden," the article pointed out that Biden is trailing the presumptive GOP nominee Donald Trump in a large majority of the latest polling.

The trend is dire, *Politico* reports. "The president's standing in head-to-head matchups with Trump is falling: Among the latest surveys this month from 13 separate pollsters, Biden's position is worse than their previous polls in all but two of them." He continues to slip in key swing states.

The outlook is now grimmer than ever, but the big divide between Biden's low popularity and public support for the Democratic Party overall was clear a year ago, despite the hype giving Biden credit for midterm election results in November 2022. Back then, the *New York Times* reported that one House Democrat offered a more candid assessment: "Biden's numbers were 'a huge drag' on Democratic candidates, who won in spite of the president not thanks to him, the lawmaker said on the condition of anonymity to avoid antagonizing the White House."

Our RootsAction.org team had no reason to avoid antagonizing the White House. Immediately after the 2022 election, we launched the Don't Run Joe campaign. Last winter, it included TV ads in New Hampshire and other early primary states as well as in D.C. We also placed full-page ads in print editions of *The Hill* newspaper, widely read on Capitol Hill; one depicted congressional Democrats as having their heads in the sand. A steady flow of news releases went out, citing data on Biden's electoral vulnerabilities. A mobile Don't Run Joe billboard circled the Capitol and White House when Congress reconvened in January.

But elected Democrats, loyal boosters and allied organizations stuck with the party line. Apparently, they couldn't imagine being independent enough to call for a candidate who could champion a progressive agenda and be a strodemocraticnger contender than the anemic Biden in the 2024 race.

Ironically, we were often told that shining a critical spotlight on Biden's re-election chances or his corporate militarism would help Donald Trump or another Republican to win in 2024. But the opposite has been the case. Biden's amen-corner enablers – going along to get along rather than risk disapproval from the White House – have been unwitting helpers of the upcoming GOP ticket.

The bleak poll numbers might actually understate the problem, as they measure only voter discontent and not activist discontent. For months next summer and fall, Democratic activists will be needed to win over undecided voters and mobilize occasional voters. But many activists who worked hard to elect Biden over Trump in 2020 now have little enthusiasm for the president, due to his policies on climate, racial justice, Gaza and other vital concerns.

After Biden formally filed as a candidate seven months ago, Don't Run Joe transitioned into Step Aside Joe. The campaign has continued to be adamant that Biden should voluntarily be a one-term president.

"The truth remains that a president is not his party's king and has no automatic right to renomination," a statement from Step Aside Joe said in April. "Simply crowning Joe Biden as the 2024 nominee is unhealthy for the Democratic Party and the country. In the face of clear polling that shows he is ill-positioned to defeat a Republican nominee, Biden is moving the Democratic Party toward a likely disaster in 2024. As the Democratic standard-bearer, Biden would represent the status quo at a time when 'wrong track' polling numbers are at an unprecedented high."

But Joe Biden and his coterie of backers continue to insist that he wear a crown. The fascistic forces behind Donald Trump are surely delighted.

Democrats Should Steer Clear of Liz Cheney

December 28, 2023

THE PUBLICATION OF LIZ CHENEY'S NEW BOOK *OATH AND Honor: A Memoir and a Warning* has thrust her back into the national spotlight. Friendly interviews with liberal TV icons like Rachel Maddow and Stephen Colbert helped the book reach the top of bestseller lists. Such enthusiasm for the former GOP representative in Democratic and liberal circles is understandable – but it's also a hazardous dynamic if Democrats want to retain the White House for another four years.

During her last term as Wyoming's representative in the House, Cheney was an admirable truthteller as she excoriated Donald Trump with key facts and deft rhetoric. Her attacks on Trump as a dire threat to American democracy rang true. But the Democratic establishment's embrace of Cheney could actually end up damaging the Biden campaign by reducing the turnout of voters who believe in the Democratic Party's core precepts.

The current problem was foreshadowed in early January 2022, when Liz Cheney's father Dick Cheney visited the House floor to mark the first anniversary of the January 6 assault on the Capitol. While showing up to support his daughter's brave anti-Trump stand, the former vice president was met with profuse accolades from top Democrats. House Speaker Nancy Pelosi went out of her way to ignore past differences, shaking the elder Cheney's hand and later telling reporters, "We were very honored by his being there."

But many Democrats don't want to see their leadership embracing prominent Republicans just because they speak out against Trump. When Liz Cheney was a member of Congress, she voted in line with President Trump 93 percent of the time. On matters like abortion rights, environmental protection, racial justice, civil liberties and national security, the younger Cheney has consistently fought for positions that the vast majority of Democrats see as inimical to the best interests of the country.

It's one thing to strive for a united front – which will be necessary –

to defeat Trump if he is the GOP nominee. But if Democratic leaders are seen as aligning themselves with Cheney, her record of voting against virtually everything that the Democratic base believes in could add to the alienation that's already felt by millions of young people who voted for Biden in 2020 but now see him as an unprincipled compromiser undeserving of their vote next year.

If Trump is the Republican nominee, Cheney will likely be a featured speaker at the Democratic National Convention, complete with a primetime TV slot. But for many Democratic voters, coziness with the likes of Cheney could be a turnoff.

If Trump is defeated in November 2024, it will not be because Democrats wooed Republican luminaries and conservative voters willing to defect from their own party. It will be because of a sufficiently large turnout from the Democratic base.

"While her work on the House Select Committee to Investigate the January 6th Attack on the U.S. Capitol has been exemplary," John Nichols noted last year, "she has an ugly history of exploiting political divisions by promoting Big Lies, as Cheney did when she refused to reject Trump's vile 'birther' lies about former President Barack Obama, and when she claimed that Vice President Kamala Harris 'sounds just like Karl Marx.'"

In fact, Cheney often sounds just like the infamous Senator Joe McCarthy and his present-day imitators Senator Lindsey Graham and Senator Ted Cruz. Her hostility toward progressives has been visceral and unrestrained, while her extreme positions are well-documented. If the Democratic Party provides her with high-profile platforms next year, the maneuver could backfire by driving away voters who are already unsure about voting for the Democratic ticket this time around.

"From backing Middle Eastern regime change to supporting an all-powerful presidency, Liz Cheney's political career has been an endless affront to democratic values – the same values she now accuses Donald Trump, her former ally, of betraying," leftist journalist Branko Marcetic writes. He points out that Cheney's political positions, including adamant support for large-scale military interventions, have been virtually identical to those of her father. Liz Cheney "was particularly excited by Trump's pledge to bring back torture, of which she was maybe the country's most vocal and ardent defender. 'Waterboarding isn't torture,' she once said, and this message was a frequent refrain for Cheney."

Liz Cheney's denunciations of Donald Trump will gain a lot of ink, pixels and airtime in 2024. And she might dissuade a relatively small number of Republicans from voting for him next fall. But many progressives could see her embrace by the Democratic leadership as evidence that the party has moved too far right to deserve their vote.

2024

For the future of the United States, this was a year of living especially dangerously. Among top Democrats, denial about Biden's evident cognitive infirmity grew along with the infirmity itself. Meanwhile, the Trump juggernaut was tearing through the Republican Party, making clear who the GOP nominee would be.

Even after Biden's disastrous debate performance in late June, the political reflex of dissembling prevented him from bowing out for another 28 days. That left the newly installed nominee Kamala Harris just 107 days to pick up the pieces before Election Day. At first, after she launched her campaign in mid-summer, it seemed that she might find ways to depart from coming across as Biden's yes-woman. But that was not to be.

Nothing epitomized the Harris campaign's moral collapse more than her insistence on echoing the Biden line about Gaza while the U.S. continued to massively arm Israel's military as it methodically killed Palestinian civilians. In the process, Harris chose to ignore both human decency and polling that showed far more voters would be likely to cast their ballots for her if she came out against sending further armaments to Israel. Disaster ensued.

U.S. ARMS UNLIMITED
STOP
IF ONLY SOMETHING COULD BE DONE.
GAZA DEATH TOLL CLIMBS
GAZA
M. WUERKER
POLITICO Andrews McMeel

Magical Thinking About Biden 2024 Paves the Way for Another Trump Presidency

January 11, 2024

AN AVALANCHE OF POLLING SHOWS JOE BIDEN WITH abysmal approval ratings and grim re-election prospects, but Democratic leaders keep spinning away in dreamland. Even before the Israeli war on Gaza began three months ago, party loyalists were in denial about Biden's unpopularity with key Democratic-leaning constituencies. Now the situation has worsened, with Biden's standing in free-fall among young people as well as Arab and Muslim Americans, while support among people of color has seriously eroded.

In a passionate letter posted last week, an anonymous group of Biden 2024 campaign staffers urged Biden to reverse himself and work for "an immediate, permanent ceasefire" in Gaza. The letter from 17 current staff members said: "Biden for President staff have seen volunteers quit in droves, and people who have voted blue for decades feel uncertain about doing so for the first time ever."

That letter echoed an appeal to Biden two months earlier – not anonymous – signed by 500 "former 2020 Biden for President and Democratic Party staff." The two unprecedented letters – and other upheaval among seasoned Democrats – have failed to snap the Democratic leadership out of their wishful, magical thinking about Biden.

Defenders of sticking with Biden glibly dismiss negative poll numbers while noting that polls in January can't tell us where persuadable voters will end up in November. But there's a serious problem beyond just polls. It's the disaffection of activists – pivotal because thousands of talented, hard-working activists are needed to help persuade voters on the fence, and to get-out-the-vote of traditional Democrats who are only "occasional voters."

During the Covid-haunted election of 2020, thousands of grassroots activists and groups – including many who were Bernie Sanders or Elizabeth Warren supporters – devoted months of their lives to defeat Donald Trump after Biden became the Democratic nominee. Overall, many progressive groups went all in for Biden when it came down to him or Trump in the fall of 2020. But in 2024, many of these experienced activists are disaffected from Biden if not outraged at him, over issues from Gaza to voting rights to climate to student debt.

In 2020, Arab and Muslim American communities mobilized against the detested, Islamophobic Trump. Today, leading activists in key swing states have been sending a clear message to Biden in public forums: "No Ceasefire, No Votes." In 2020, climate activists mobilized to eject the climate-denying "drill baby drill" incumbent. Today, as a result of Biden's reversals on climate policy – like his broken promise on drilling in Alaska – there is much disgust among activists.

Five hundred people who were campaign or party staff members in 2020 – recalling that they "fought tirelessly to organize millions of Americans to cast their votes" for Biden – have now signed a well-informed letter urging Biden not only to work for a Gaza ceasefire, but also to "end unconditional military aid to Israel" and "take concrete steps to end the conditions of apartheid, occupation, and ethnic cleansing that are the root causes of this devastation."

Will there be enough diligent volunteers to get-out-the-vote for Biden in 2024? Not according to current Biden for President staffers who say volunteers have "quit in droves" over Biden's handling of the Gaza war – adding: "It is not enough to merely be the alternative to Donald Trump."

For more than a year, I've been part of the RootsAction team that launched the Don't Run Joe (now Step Aside Joe) campaign immediately after the 2022 midterm elections – urging progressives to insist on clearing the path for an open primary process that could lead to a dynamic progressive candidate capable of soundly defeating Trump. Now, the awful specter of a Biden vs. Trump contest is causing enormous distress and eagerness to develop an appropriate response.

While establishment Democrats are intent on whistling past the Biden graveyard, there's a different kind of magical thinking among some who consider themselves to be on the left – a fantastical pretense that it doesn't really matter whether Trump becomes president again. People who think that Trump and his leadership team are not fascistic, or that a Trumpite return to the presidency wouldn't be much worse than abhorrent Bidenism, are out of touch with political reality.

Dodging Biden's Moral Collapse Is No Way to Defeat Trump

February 14, 2024

FOR MORE THAN FOUR MONTHS, PRESIDENT BIDEN HAS BEEN the main enabler for Israel's mass murder of Palestinian people in Gaza. Every day, hundreds of civilians are killed by U.S. weaponry and, increasingly, by hunger and disease. The cruelty and magnitude of the slaughter are repugnant to anyone who isn't somehow numb to the human agony.

Such numbing is widespread in the United States. Some factors include ethnocentric, racial and religious biases against Arabs and Muslims. The steep pro-Israel tilt of news media runs parallel to the slant of U.S. government officials, with language that routinely conveys much lower regard for Palestinian lives than Israeli lives.

And while the credibility of the Israeli government has tumbled, the brawny arms of the Israel lobby – notably AIPAC and Democratic Majority for Israel – still exert enormous leverage over the vast majority of Congress. Few legislators are willing to vote against massive military aid that makes the carnage in Gaza possible.

A chilling example is Senator Chris Van Hollen of Maryland. On Monday night, he took to the Senate floor and condemned Israel in no uncertain terms. "Kids in Gaza are now dying from the deliberate withholding of food," he said. "In addition to the horror of that news, one other thing is true. That is a war crime. It is a textbook war crime. And that makes those who orchestrate it war criminals."

Watching video from Van Hollen's impassioned speech, you might assume that he would vote against sending $14 billion in further military aid to those "war criminals." But hours later, he did just the opposite. As journalist Ryan Grim noted, "the senator's speech pulsed with moral clarity – until it petered out into a stumbling rationale for his forthcoming yes vote."

In contrast, three senators in the Democratic caucus – Jeff Merkley, Peter Welch and Bernie Sanders – voted no. Sanders delivered a powerful speech calling for decency instead of further moral collapse from the top of the U.S. government.

While the Senate deliberated, the White House again made clear that it wasn't serious about getting in the way of Israel's planned assault on the city of Rafah. That's where most of Gaza's 2.2 million surviving residents have taken unsafe refuge from the Orwellian-named Israel Defense Forces.

An exchange at a White House news conference on Monday underscored that Biden is determined to keep enabling Israel's continuous war crimes in Gaza:

> **Reporter:** "Has the president ever threatened to strip military assistance from Israel if they move ahead with a Rafah operation that does not take into consequence what happens with civilians?"
>
> **Spokesman John Kirby:** "We're going to continue to support Israel. They have a right to defend themselves against Hamas and we're going to continue to make sure they have the tools and the capabilities to do that."

Later this week, *Politico* summed up: "The Biden administration is not planning to punish Israel if it launches a military campaign in Rafah without ensuring civilian safety." Citing interviews with three U.S. officials, the article reported that "no reprimand plans are in the works, meaning Israeli forces could enter the city and harm civilians without facing American consequences."

Biden continues to serve as an accomplice while mouthing platitudes of concern about the lives of civilians in Gaza. Month after month, he has done all he can to supply the Israeli military to the max.

Under an apt headline – "Biden Is Mad at Netanyahu? Spare Me." – *The Nation* senior editor Jack Mirkinson wrote this week: "In the real world, Biden and his legislative partners have continued to arm Israel; the Democratic leadership in the Senate actually brought people in on Super Bowl Sunday to take a vote on a bill that would, along with rearming Ukraine, send Israel another $14.1 billion for what is euphemistically dubbed 'security assistance.'"

Ever since October, inspiring protests and activism in the United States have challenged U.S. support for Israel's military assault on Gaza. However, boosted by revulsion at the atrocities that Hamas committed against Israeli civilians on October 7, the usual rationales for supporting Israel's violence against Palestinians have been hard at work.

In this election year, an additional factor looms large. With just eight months until the voting starts that could propel Donald Trump back into the presidency, the prospect of his return to power is all too real. And with Biden set to be the Democratic Party's nominee, countless individuals and groups are careful to avoid saying much that's critical of the president they want to see re-elected.

Instead of candor, the routine choices have been euphemisms and silence. But – morally and politically – that's a big mistake.

The electoral base that Biden is going to need for re-election is heavily against his support for Israel's war on Gaza. Polling shows that young people in particular are overwhelmingly opposed. Most have seen through the thin veneer of his weak pleas for Israel to not kill so many civilians.

No amount of evasions, silences or doubletalk can make Biden's policies morally acceptable. But – while the administration combines its PR hand-wringing with military arms-supplying – Biden apologists go on and on with evasion and verbal gymnastics to defend the indefensible.

A far better course of action would be actual candor about current realities: Joe Biden's moral collapse is enabling the Israeli government to continue, with impunity, its large-scale massacre of Palestinian people. In the process, Biden is increasing the chances that the Republican Party, led by fascistic Donald Trump, will gain control of the White House in January.

Who You Gonna Believe, Biden Loyalists or Your Own Eyes and Ears?

July 1, 2024

ALMOST AS APPALLING AS PRESIDENT BIDEN'S DEBATE performance are the efforts of his loyalists to pretend that what 50 million viewers saw and heard didn't happen or didn't really matter. What has unfolded in the last few days amounts to a political gaslighting operation by the Biden campaign and supportive pretenders who've been trying to erase history as soon as it happened.

Apparently, Biden's ego has proven to be much more resilient than his cognition, while loved ones and sycophants in concentric inner and outer circles cling desperately to talking points that are patently dishonest, often preposterous, and virulently dangerous for prospects of preventing a second Trump presidency.

By whistling past the graveyard of Biden's credibility as a viable candidate in 2024, the pretenders are doing a huge disservice to all who want to avert a full takeover of the U.S. government by the fascistic Republican Party.

Let's start with the innermost circle – the First Couple. The day after the debate, both sidestepped what it had shown, instead striving to make it about one man's quest to show individual resilience.

"I know like millions of Americans know – when you get knocked down, you get back up," the president told rallygoers in North Carolina. Meeting in New York with donors, Jill Biden said: "When Joe gets knocked down, Joe gets back up, and that's what we're doing today."

Jill Biden's role goes far beyond the personal with her husband. After Biden became president, *Vogue* described his wife as "a key player in her husband's administration, a West Wing surrogate and policy advocate."

But it's worth asking what kind of "key player" could tell President Biden immediately after his disastrous debate performance, as Jill Biden did late Thursday night: "Joe, you did such a great job! You answered every question! You knew all the facts!"

Party leadership was worse than dubious when, following the debate, House Democratic power broker Representative James Clyburn of South Carolina intoned: "Let's just stay the course." And when a former Democratic president, Barack Obama, dismissively declared on X: "Bad debate nights happen."

A master class in evasion and obfuscation came moments after the debate ended when California Governor Gavin Newsom went on MSNBC to exhibit his damage-control skills. The damage was beyond repair, but he did his best.

"On the signature issue the Democrats have, which is abortion, the president's response was garbled and undirected at best," a reporter pointed out. "Do you feel like he did what he needed to do on an issue that could motivate voters?"

"I think it's significantly insignificant, because it's de minimis, because the American people have made up their minds," Newsom replied. "They don't support the policies of Donald Trump" on abortion.

Newsom went on: "We have the opportunity to universally have the back of this president, who's had our back. You don't turn your back, you go home with the one that brought you to the dance. A hundred percent. All in. And I was very very proud that he was able to articulate the work that he has done, and lay a foundation of understanding of the lies and the deceit that continue to come out of Donald Trump's mouth."

The day after the debate, interviewed by Al Sharpton on MSNBC, the Democratic National Committee's chair Jaime Harrison – who serves at Biden's pleasure – echoed Newsom's carefully obtuse rhetoric, proclaiming that "Joe Biden has always had our back, and we're gonna have his."

Meanwhile, liberal mega-substacker Heather Cox Richardson absurdly extended her longstanding record as a scholarly shill for President Biden by writing: "Biden needed to demonstrate that his mental capacity is strong in order to push back on the Republicans' insistence that he is incapable of being president. That, he did, thoroughly. Biden began with a weak start but hit his stride as the evening wore on. Indeed, he covered his bases too thoroughly, listing the many accomplishments of his administration in such a hurry that he was sometimes hard to understand."

But such intellectually disingenuous claims have suddenly worn thin in a wide range of media. Habitual supporters of Biden, such as Joe Scarborough at MSNBC and Thomas Friedman at the *New York Times*, responded to his abysmal effort in the debate by calling for him to drop out of the race. The *Times* editorial board did the same. During the last few days, a vast array of mainstream outlets featured urgent calls for Biden to withdraw as a candidate.

But the prominent Democrats now refusing to acknowledge that Biden was awful in the debate also refuse to acknowledge that he has been directly aiding mass murder of Palestinians in Gaza. That's what happens when deference to a leader substitutes fealty for humanity.

Last weekend, my colleague Sam Rosenthal wrote about his experience of flyering for RootsAction's Step Aside Joe campaign at a meeting of the Democratic National Committee in early 2023: "How did DNC members, staffers, and media attendees react to our open display of dissent? About how you would expect – most ignored us, a few others mocked us, one or two even angrily confronted our ragtag group."

On Sunday, *USA Today* described the results of a new poll: "72 percent of voters do not believe Biden has the mental or cognitive health to serve as president, as well as nearly half of his own party. That's up seven points from the beginning of June."

But at the same time those poll results were released, former Biden White House chief of staff Ron Klain "said that it was 100 percent certain the president would stay in the race," the *New York Times* reported. Fingers stuck firmly in his ears, Klain commented: "He is the choice of the Democratic voters. We are seeing record levels of support from grassroots donors. We had a bad debate night. But you win campaigns by fighting – not quitting – in the face of adversity."

More Than Ever, Trump's Most Effective Campaign Ally Is Joe Biden

July 5, 2024

WHEN JOE BIDEN'S ABC NEWS INTERVIEW AIRED ON FRIDAY night, it made clear that he should not be running for re-election. Rather than reduce the concerns sparked by his abysmal debate performance eight days earlier, the interview underscored that the president is in denial about his current political standing and unable to offer reassurance that his mental capacities are unimpaired.

Notably, Biden kept dodging and refusing to reply in the affirmative when journalist George Stephanopoulos asked whether he has had "a full neurological and cognitive evaluation" and if he would "be willing to have the independent medical evaluation."

While insisting that his behavior during the debate was "no indication of any serious condition," Biden evaded key questions while resorting to snippets of stump speeches emphasizing purported foreign-policy "successes." The interview transcript makes for ominous reading. If Joe Biden is the candidate standing between America and a second Trump presidency, the nation is in extremely dire straits.

Four years after the Democratic Party and grassroots activists propelled Biden into the presidency, he is now adamant that he'll stay the course as the 2024 nominee – in effect, greatly boosting the Republican Party's prospects for winning control of the White House and Congress.

It was widely reported that Joe Biden told more than 20 Democratic governors on Wednesday that he needs more sleep and that events should not be scheduled for him after 8 pm. Democrats have reason to question whether Biden is capable of mounting a vigorous presidential campaign; swing voters may wonder if he can run the White House.

It's all too tempting to lapse into spectator mode as developments in the current Biden psychodrama unfold. But progressives and others who understand the imperative of preventing a second Trump term should be determined to help shape history rather than just watching it in real time.

In recent days, it has become clear that only direct intervention by Democrats in Congress, propelled by grassroots pressure, can avert a Biden 2024 train wreck. It's time to pull the emergency cord. And that means constituents should deluge every congressional Democrat with demands that they insist on Biden's withdrawal from the presidential race.

This telling exchange occurred near the end of the interview:

> **STEPHANOPOULOS:** "If you are told reliably from your allies, from your friends and supporters in the Democratic Party in the House and the Senate that they're concerned you're gonna lose the House and the Senate if you stay in, what will you do?"

> **BIDEN:** "I'm not gonna answer that question. It's not gonna happen."

Proving Biden wrong on that point will be essential.

Biden's frequent dalliance with magical thinking rather than realism makes him the most powerful de facto ally that Donald Trump has in his quest to regain the White House.

Deference to Joe Biden from Bernie Sanders Has Become Nonsensical

July 8, 2024

I LOVE BERNIE SANDERS. BY MOST MEASURES, HE'S THE greatest senator in the last 50 years. I was very glad to be a Sanders delegate to the 2016 and 2020 Democratic National Conventions. But when Bernie screws up, his progressive base should say so.

That happened during the first months of Israel's war on Gaza that began last October. Initially, Bernie sounded equivocal as Israeli forces engaged in mass murder. After several weeks of carnage, antiwar activists occupied his D.C. office to demand support for a ceasefire. Some were arrested for their civil disobedience.

Bernie gradually changed his position and became a fierce critic of Israel, denouncing it for horrific large-scale crimes against Palestinian civilians and challenging the shipment of weapons to the Israeli military. There's no telling if the public pressure from progressives hastened his shift to strongly oppose Israel's genocidal war. But that pressure was necessary.

Unfortunately, after President Biden's debate debacle on June 27, Bernie did not weigh in against the gaslighting maneuvers by the White House and the Biden campaign. In fact, Bernie aided them by downplaying the importance of what had happened on the debate stage.

Since then, Bernie has encouraged the illusion that Biden now has the capacity to be an effective candidate against Donald Trump. Equally problematic has been the implicit pretense that Biden could be up to the job as president until January 2029.

Such evasion not only dodges the reality that Biden was inept and sometimes incoherent during the debate. Since then, much stunning information has come to light, illuminating how badly Biden's mental capacities have diminished.

"In the weeks and months before President Biden's politically devastating performance on the debate stage in Atlanta, several current and former officials and others who encountered him behind closed doors noticed that he increasingly appeared confused or listless, or would lose the thread of conversations," the *New York Times* reported on July 2.

But on July 3 and again on July 5, email from Bernie to supporters told them: "President Biden said today that he is staying in the race, and I take him at his word." However, taking Biden "at his word" is beside the point. As the party's nominee, Biden would drag down many Democratic candidates with him while making it easy for Donald Trump to win the presidency again. The problem isn't only what Bernie has been telling people on his email list. He has also been putting out important messages to the broader public via mass media – in the process sending positive signals to Biden and his top aides while they gauge whether to continue the Biden 2024 campaign.

And Bernie is talking directly with the president. Biden "has spoken to me in recent days," Bernie said on Sunday during an interview on the CBS program "Face the Nation." It's very likely that what Bernie told Biden was consistent with what he told The Associated Press, which reported on July 2 that Sanders "does not want Biden to step aside."

The AP quoted Bernie as saying: "A presidential election is not a Grammy Award contest for the best singer or entertainer. It's about who has the best policies that impact our lives."

But Biden's inability to clearly advocate for popular policies – or to effectively refute lies and demagogic statements from Donald Trump – is not like a failure to be "the best singer or entertainer." The president's glaring inabilities amount to huge failures as a candidate and as a leader.

It's well known that Bernie Sanders has personal warmth toward Joe Biden. But, given the enormity of what is at stake, personal ties should not get in the way of realizing what ought to be crystal clear: Every day that goes by with Joe Biden as the presumptive Democratic nominee will work to the further advantage of Trump and his extremist right-wing forces.

"I'm going to do everything I can to see that Biden gets re-elected," Bernie told The Associated Press. But at this juncture, that's the wrong vow. What we really need to hear from Bernie Sanders is a pledge to do everything he can to see that Trump is defeated – and that means replacing Biden with someone who has a better chance of getting the job done.

The Democratic Party's Culture of Loyalty: How an Ethos of Compliance Made the Biden Debacle Possible

July 25, 2024

THE BIDEN CAMPAIGN DROVE THE DEMOCRATIC PARTY INTO A ditch and speculation is rampant about grim prospects for the election. But little scrutiny has gone into examining how such a dire situation developed in the first place.

A culture of dubious loyalty festered far beyond the Biden White House. It encompassed Democratic leaders at the Capitol and across the country, as well as countless allied organizations and individuals. The routine was to pretend that Biden's obvious cognitive deficits didn't exist or didn't really matter.

Because his mental impairment was so apparent to debate viewers, some notable Democratic dissenters in Congress stepped up to oppose his renomination. But for weeks, relatively few colleagues followed the lead of Texas Representative Lloyd Doggett, who broke the congressional ice by calling for Biden to "make the painful and difficult decision to withdraw."

– – – –

Acuity came from Julián Castro, former secretary of Housing and Urban Development in the Obama administration, who kept up a barrage of cogent tweets. One message referred to Biden's "unique political liability" and warned: "It's not going to get any better – and has a high risk of scrambling the race again, sealing Dems fate. Burying our heads in the sand won't assuage voters concerns, which have been painfully obvious for years."

A literal heads-in-the-sand photo was at the top of a full-page print ad that the Don't Run Joe team at RootsAction (where I'm national director) placed in The Hill a year and a half ago. Headlined "An Open Letter to Democrats in the House and Senate," it said: "Many of your colleagues, and maybe you, are expressing public enthusiasm for another Biden presidential campaign in on-the-record quotes to journalists – while privately voicing trepidation. This widespread gap ill serves the party or the nation... There are ample indications that having Joe Biden at the top of ballots across the country in autumn 2024 would bring enormous political vulnerabilities for the ticket and for down-ballot races. No amount of spin can change key realities."

But the spin never stopped and, in fact, went into high gear this summer with Biden trying to make his candidacy a fait accompli. Meanwhile, the culture of loyalty kept a grip on the delegates who'll be heading to Chicago in mid-August for the Democratic National Convention. As the second week of July began, CNN reported that "a host of party leaders and rank-and-file members selected to formally nominate Biden said they were loath to consider any other option." A delegate from Florida put it this way: "There is no plan B. The president is the nominee. And that's where I and everyone that I've been talking to stands – until and unless he says otherwise."

The lure of going along to get along with high-ranking officials is part of the Democratic Party's dominant political culture. I saw such dynamics up close, countless times, during my 10 years as a member of the California Democratic Party's state central committee, and as a delegate to three Democratic National Conventions. I viewed such conformist attitudes with alarm at meetings of the Democratic National Committee.

Larry Cohen, former president of the Communications Workers of America, has been on the DNC since 2005. "Currently the national Democratic Party exists in name only, and is largely the White House and a nominating procedure for the president," he told me. "The internal life is in the 57 state and territorial parties, and important reform efforts are visible in many of them." Cohen added: "It's the 'rules and not just the rulers,' and the Democratic Party compares poorly to centrist parties in other democracies, especially with the domination of corporate and billionaire money in our nominating process at every level of government."

Pia Gallegos, co-founder and former chair of the Adelante Progressive Caucus of the New Mexico Democratic Party, summed it up this way: "The culture of the Democratic Party at the national level is top-down in the sense that it appoints the members of its committees rather than opens committee membership to elections among the DNC delegates – and then expects its delegates to rubber-stamp approval of those appointments."

Gallegos, who chairs the board of RootsAction, is on the steering committee of the nationwide State Democratic Party Progressives Network, an independent group that formed last year. "Democratic parties at the state level also have policies or traditions to appoint local committee members or national committee representatives, consequentially pushing out their more progressive or reformist members from positions of power," she said. In short, "the Democratic Party leadership appears to be more concerned with maintaining their control of the party than with promoting democracy within the party."

When it comes to their decision-making, some state parties have headed in more democratic directions – or the opposite. I've seen first-hand that the nation's largest one, the California Democratic Party, has steadily become more autocratic for over a decade.

Overall, big donors and entrenched power are propelling the Democratic Party.

After Judith Whitmer became an active DNC member as chair of the Nevada Democratic Party, she got a close look at the committee's inner workings. "Today's Democratic Party is run by consultants and operatives who tightly control every aspect of the DNC," she texted me. "The big-tent party that champions 'democracy' is actually a small circle of insiders who hold all the power by maintaining the status quo. Dissenting opinions are not welcome. Progressives are ostracized, and the everyday voter no longer has a voice."

In early 2021, a progressive insurgent campaign enabled Whitmer to be elected chair of Nevada's Democratic Party. Powerful Democrats in the state, outmaneuvered by that grassroots organizing, quickly transferred $450,000 from the Nevada party's coffers to the Democratic Senatorial Campaign Committee and set up a parallel state organization. Two years later, the erstwhile party establishment retaliated by crushing Whitmer's re-election bid.

– – – –

Subduing progressive power is a key goal of dominant party leaders as they gauge when and where to strike. While nominally supporting the two-term progressive Congressman Jamaal Bowman for re-election in his New York district last month, powerful party elders nonetheless winked and nodded as AIPAC poured some $15 million into backing a corporate pro-war Democrat against him.

"The Democratic Party is, in one word, simply undemocratic," Joseph Geevarghese, executive director of the national activist group Our Revolution, told me. "The illusion of 'party unity' fostered by Biden and Bernie [Sanders] four years ago is gone. In fact, the donor class feels emboldened to wage war openly with progressives, especially after defeating Jamaal Bowman."

I saw the illusion of party unity playing out at sessions of the Unity Reform Commission that the DNC convened in 2017. The calculus was that the strength of Bernie Sanders forces, then at high ebb, had to be reckoned with. The commission had a slight but decisive majority of members aligned with Hillary Clinton, while the rest of the seats went to allies of Sanders. While the commission did adopt some modest reforms, the majority balked at substantive DNC rules changes that would have provided financial transparency or prevented serious conflicts of interest.

Overseeing the blockage of those changes was Jennifer O'Malley Dillon, the commission chair, who later worked for three years as deputy chief of staff in Joe Biden's White House. She went on to become the Biden campaign chair.

"The Democratic Party now functions through foundation-funded advocacy organizations, and without the kind of self-funded mass membership groups that had a genuine voice with real power when the labor and civil rights movements were strong," journalist David Dayen wrote in early July for The American Prospect. "If you read the polls, the interests of the public and the donor class are actually aligned in favor of Biden's withdrawal. But given who's making that case, it sure doesn't feel that way, nor does it feel particularly small-d democratic. That makes it easy for Biden to fall back on the will of 'the people' who voted in Democratic Potemkin primaries, because outside of that, the people are voiceless."

– – – –

Alan Minsky, executive director of Progressive Democrats of America, had this to say when I asked him to describe the party's political culture: "While the Democratic Party is a complex organization with a lot of dimensions, I think the role of money – and, more specifically, the never-ending need to raise more money – has become its central organizing principle. This, of course, skews the priorities of the party in a conservative direction. Democrats who can raise money comparable to the levels raised by the GOP are seen as indispensable to the party, and grow in power and influence… In turn, these powerful money-raising Democrats have little use for anyone inside the party who is perceived as jeopardizing the flow of money – such as left-progressives and other advocates for the poor and working class."

Minsky added:

> "As these dynamics became central to the party over the past few decades, the rich and powerful grew in influence, and the general political culture reflected the priorities of the professional class rather than the working class, a sharp contrast to the mid-20th century, which was the height of the party's power and influence.

> "However, since the GOP only turns ever more to the right, progressives and working-class advocates continue to stake a claim in the Democratic Party. Paradoxically, since these non-wealthy groups represent the majority of the population, they also provide the best opportunity for the party to regain its majority status. However, from the point of view of the party's dominant faction, and their legions of highly compensated consultants, this is an unacceptable outcome as it would shut down the gravy train."

The Democratic National Committee building on South Capitol Street in Washington is a monument to the funding prowess of multi-billionaire Haim Saban, who became the chair of the capital campaign in late 2001 to raise $32 million for the new headquarters. He quickly donated $7 million to the DNC, believed to be the largest political donation ever made until then.

Saban has long been close to Bill and Hillary Clinton. By 2016, Mother Jones reported, Saban and his wife Cheryl – in addition to hosting "lucrative fundraisers" – had given "upward of $27 million to assorted Clinton causes and campaigns."

Saban and Joe Biden also bonded. When Saban had an appointment at the White House last September, "the visit was supposed to last an hour, as part of lunch, but in practice he spent three hours with the president and his people," the Israeli newspaper Yediot Ahronoth reported.

Reasons to reaffirm warm relations with the likes of Haim Saban were obvious. Presumably, the president remembered that a single virtual fundraiser the Sabans put together for the Biden-Harris campaign in September 2020 brought in $4.5 million. In February 2024, with the Gaza slaughter in its 135th day, the Sabans hosted a re-election fundraiser for the president at their home in Los Angeles. The price of a ticket ranged from $3,300 to $250,000. An ardent Zionist, Saban has repeatedly said: "I'm a one-issue guy, and my issue is Israel."

This summer, while Biden fought to retain his spot as nominee, fervent support from the Congressional Black Caucus seemed pivotal. The CBC has changed markedly since the 1970s and 1980s, when its leadership came from visionary representatives like Shirley Chisholm, John Conyers, and Ron Dellums. Then, the caucus was antiwar and wary of corporate power. Now, it's overwhelmingly pro-war and in willing captivity to corporate America.

With President Biden in distinct denial about his unfitness to run again, the role of the Congressional Progressive Caucus was accommodating. Its chair, Pramila Jayapal, endorsed him for 2024 gratuitously early – in November 2022 – declaring herself "a convert." Since then, some high-profile progressives went out of their way to back Biden in his determination to run for re-election.

Representative Alexandria Ocasio-Cortez, who endorsed Biden a year ago, went in front of journalists 10 days after his debate disaster to make a vehement pitch for him as the nominee. In a similar mode, Senator Bernie Sanders was notably outspoken for Biden to stay on as the party's standard-bearer, even implausibly claiming on national television that, with a proper message, "he's going to win, and win big."

When some of the best progressive members of Congress fall under the spell of such contorted loyalty, it's an indication that deference to the leadership of the Democratic Party has come at much too high a price.

The Ghost of Hubert Humphrey Is Stalking Kamala Harris

August 15, 2024

AFTER THE DEMOCRAT IN THE WHITE HOUSE DECIDED NOT TO run for re-election, the vice president got the party's presidential nod – and continued to back the administration's policies for an unpopular war. As the election neared, the candidate had to decide whether to keep supporting the war or speak out for a change.

Hubert Humphrey faced that choice in 1968. Kamala Harris faces it now.

Despite the differences in eras and circumstances, key dynamics are eerily similar. The history of how Vice President Humphrey navigated the political terrain of the war in Vietnam has ominous parallels with how Vice President Harris has been dealing with the war in Gaza.

– – – –

For millions of liberals, during the first half of the 1960s, Hubert Humphrey was the nation's most heroic politician. As the Senate majority whip, he deftly championed landmark bills for civil rights and social programs. By the time President Lyndon B. Johnson put him on the Democratic ticket in 1964, progressive momentum was in high gear.

LBJ defeated ultra-conservative Barry Goldwater in a landslide. As vice president, Humphrey assisted Johnson to follow up on the 1964 Civil Rights Act with the 1965 Voting Rights Act and a huge set of antipoverty measures while enacting broad social programs in realms of education, healthcare, nutrition, housing and the environment. Midway through the summer of 1965, Johnson signed Medicare and Medicaid into law.

Meanwhile, escalation of the U.S. war on Vietnam was taking off. And, as Martin Luther King Jr. soon pointed out, "When a nation becomes obsessed with the guns of war, social programs must inevitably suffer. We can talk about guns and butter all we want to, but when the guns are there with all of its emphasis you don't even get good oleo [margarine]. These are facts of life."

At first, Vice President Humphrey wrote slightly dovish memos to Johnson, who angrily rejected the advice and retaliated by excluding him from key meetings. Banished to the doghouse, Humphrey licked his wounds and changed his approach. By early 1966, he was deferring to Johnson's war views in private and advocating for the Vietnam War in public.

As the war escalated, so did the vice president's zeal to extol it as a fight for freedom and democracy. "By 1967 he had become a hawk on Vietnam," biographer Arnold Offner noted. Beneath the lofty rhetoric was cold calculation.

"Humphrey's passage from dove to hawk on Vietnam was not the result of one-sided White House briefings or of his ability, as one journalist had noted, to see silver linings in the stormiest clouds," Offner wrote. "His change of position derived from a case of willful mind over matter, from his strong anti-Communism combined with political expediency driven by ambition, namely desire to remain in Johnson's good graces and perhaps succeed him whenever his presidency ended."

That desire to be in the president's good graces did not dissipate after Johnson suddenly announced in a televised address on March 31, 1968 that he would not seek re-election. Four weeks later, Humphrey launched a presidential campaign that pitted him against two antiwar candidates, Senators Eugene McCarthy and Robert Kennedy.

From the outset, Humphrey was plagued by his fear of antagonizing Johnson if he were to depart from a pro-war script. The United States had "nothing to apologize for," Humphrey said. He didn't run in any primaries and was not willing to debate McCarthy or Kennedy.

Humphrey mouthed the same old rhetoric to rationalize the administration's policies for the war in Vietnam. Several high-level supporters – including Iowa's Governor Harold Hughes, Vermont's Governor Philip Hoff, and the venerable former New York governor and ambassador Averell Harriman – advised him to resign the vice presidency and thus free himself from entanglement with Johnson. But to Humphrey, such a step was unthinkable.

And so, Hubert Humphrey rode in the caboose of the war train all summer. In late August, the day before the Democratic National Convention got underway in Chicago, he told viewers of the CBS program "Face the Nation" that the administration's policies in Vietnam were "basically sound."

The convention nominated him while, outside, tear gas filled the air during what a report from a special federal commission later called a police riot that meted out violence to antiwar demonstrators as well as some journalists. Inside the turbulent convention, dissenting delegates were outshouted, outvoted and suppressed by the pro-Humphrey forces.

The chaos and bitterness in Chicago underscored how the vice president's deference to the war president had weakened the party while undermining the chances for victory. In polls, Humphrey trailed the Republican candidate Richard Nixon by double digits.

And yet, like a true warhorse, the VP could not bring himself to break from the president's steely insistence on maintaining the U.S. government's horrific violence in Vietnam. The Democratic ticket of Humphrey and Maine's Senator Edmund Muskie was in a tailspin, propelled downward by Humphrey's refusal to break ranks with Johnson.

It wasn't until September 30 that Humphrey took a meaningful step. His campaign bought 30 minutes of national TV air time on NBC, and he used it to deliver a speech that finally created a bit of daylight between him and Johnson's war. Humphrey said that as president he'd be willing to halt the bombing of North Vietnam. The speech revived his campaign, which nearly closed the gap with Nixon in October. But it was too little, too late.

– – – –

Like Hubert Humphrey six decades ago, Kamala Harris has remained in step with the man responsible for changing her title from senator to vice president. She has toed President Biden's war line, while at times voicing sympathy for the victims of the Gaza war that's made possible by policies that she supports. Her words of compassion have yet to translate into opposing the pipeline of weapons and ammunition to the Israeli military as it keeps slaughtering Palestinian civilians.

As the Democratic standard-bearer during carnage in Gaza, Harris has been trying to square a circle of mass murder, expressing empathy for victims while staying within bounds of U.S. government policies. Last week, Harris had her national security adviser declare that "she does not support an arms embargo on Israel."

If maintained, that stance will continue to be a moral catastrophe – while increasing the chances that Harris will lose to Donald Trump. In effect, so far, Harris has opted to stay aligned with power brokers, big donors and conventional political wisdom instead of aligning with most voters. A CBS News / YouGov poll in June found that Americans opposed sending "weapons and supplies to Israel" by 61 to 39 percent.

Last week, Harris described herself and running-mate Tim Walz as "joyful warriors." Many outlets have heralded their joyride along the campaign trail. The Associated Press reported that "Harris is pushing joy." A *New York Times* headline proclaimed that "joy is fueling her campaign." The brand of the Harris campaign is fast becoming "the politics of joy."

Such branding will be a sharp contrast to the outcries from thousands of protesters in Chicago outside the Democratic National Convention next week, as they denounce U.S. complicity with the killing of so many children, women and other civilians in Gaza.

Campaigning for joy while supporting horrendous warfare is nothing new. Fifty-six years before Vice President Harris called herself a "joyful warrior," Vice President Humphrey declared that he stood for the "politics of joy" when announcing his run for the 1968 Democratic presidential nomination.

At that point, the Pentagon was several years into its massive killing spree in Vietnam, as Humphrey kicked off his campaign by saying: "here we are the spirit of dedication, here we are the way politics ought to be in America, the politics of happiness, politics of purpose, politics of joy; and that's the way it's going to be, all the way, too, from here on out."

If Kamala Harris loses to Trump after sticking with her support for arming the slaughter in Gaza, historians will likely echo words from biographer Offner, who wrote that after the 1968 election Humphrey "asked himself repeatedly whether he should have distanced himself sooner from President Johnson on the war. The answer was all too obvious."

Biden's Convention Speech Made Absurd Claims About His Gaza Policy

August 20, 2024

AN OBSERVATION FROM GEORGE ORWELL – "THOSE WHO control the present, control the past and those who control the past control the future" – is acutely relevant to how President Biden talked about Gaza during his speech at the Democratic convention Monday night. His words fit into a messaging template now in its eleventh month, depicting the U.S. government as tirelessly seeking peace, while supplying the weapons and bombs that have enabled Israel's continual slaughter of civilians.

"We'll keep working, to bring hostages home, and end the war in Gaza, and bring peace and security to the Middle East," Biden told the cheering delegates. "As you know, I wrote a peace treaty for Gaza. A few days ago I put forward a proposal that brought us closer to doing that than we've done since October 7th."

It was a journey into an alternative universe of political guile from a president who just six days earlier had approved sending $20 billion worth of more weapons to Israel. Yet the Biden delegates in the convention hall responded with a crescendo of roaring admiration.

Applause swelled as Biden continued: "We're working around-the-clock, my secretary of state, to prevent a wider war and reunite hostages with their families, and surge humanitarian health and food assistance into Gaza now, to end the civilian suffering of the Palestinian people and finally, finally, finally deliver a ceasefire and end this war."

In Chicago's United Center, the president basked in adulation while claiming to be a peacemaker despite a record of literally making possible the methodical massacres of tens of thousands of Palestinian civilians.

Orwell would have understood. A political reflex has been in motion from top U.S. leaders, claiming to be peace seekers while aiding and abetting the slaughter. Normalizing deception about the past sets a pattern for perpetrating such deception in the future.

And so, working inside the paradigm that Orwell described, Biden exerts control over the present, strives to control narratives about the past, and seeks to make it all seem normal, prefiguring the future.

The eagerness of delegates to cheer for Biden's mendaciously absurd narrative about his administration's policies toward Gaza was in a broader context – the convention's lovefest for the lame-duck president.

Hours before the convention opened, Peter Beinart released a short video essay anticipating the fervent adulation. "I just don't think when you're analyzing a presidency or a person, you sequester what's happened in Gaza," he said. "I mean, if you're a liberal-minded person, you believe that genocide is just about the worst thing that a country can do, and it's just about the worst thing that your country can do if your country is arming a genocide."

Beinart continued:

> And it's really not that controversial anymore that this qualifies as a genocide. I read the academic writing on this. I don't see any genuine scholars of human rights international law who are saying it's not indeed there.... If you're gonna say something about Joe Biden, the president, Joe Biden, the man, you have to factor in what Joe Biden, the president, Joe Biden, the man, has done, vis-a-vis Gaza. It's central to his legacy. It's central to his character. And if you don't, then you're saying that Palestinian lives just don't matter, or at least they don't matter this particular day, and I think that's inhumane. I don't think we can ever say that some group of people's lives simply don't matter because it's inconvenient for us to talk about them at a particular moment.

Underscoring the grotesque moral obtuseness from the convention stage was the joyful display of generations as the president praised and embraced his offspring. Joe Biden walked off stage holding the hand of his cute little grandson, a precious child no more precious than any one of the many thousands of children the president has helped Israel to kill.

In CNN Interview, Harris Dodged Gaza Genocide and Damaged Her Election Prospects

August 30, 2024

TIME IS RUNNING OUT FOR KAMALA HARRIS TO DISTANCE herself from U.S. policies that enable Israel to continue with mass murder and genocide in Gaza. Polling shows that a pivot toward moral decency would improve her chances of defeating Donald Trump. But during her CNN interview Thursday night, Harris remained in lockstep with President Biden's unconditional arming of Israel.

Two weeks ago, YouGov pollsters released findings in Arizona, Georgia and Pennsylvania, three swing states now on a razor's edge between Harris and Trump. "In Pennsylvania, 34 percent of respondents said they would be more likely to vote for the Democratic nominee if the nominee vowed to withhold weapons to Israel, compared to 7 percent who said they would be less likely. The rest said it would make no difference," the new journalism site Zeteo reported.

Results in the two other states were similar. "In Arizona, 35 percent said they'd be more likely, while 5 percent would be less likely. And in Georgia, 39 percent said they'd be more likely, also compared to 5 percent who would be less likely."

But on CNN, Harris stuck to echoing Biden's rhetoric – calling for a ceasefire while dodging the reality that the U.S. government could force one by implementing an arms embargo on Israel.

Huge U.S. shipments of weapons and bombs to Israel keep allowing it to massacre and starve civilians of all ages while violating federal statutes as well as international law. Days ago, Biden approved sending arms to Israel worth upwards of $20 billion. The transfers were called "sales," but as policy analyst Stephen Semler pointed out, "most if not all of this matériel is paid for by U.S. taxpayers – Israel uses much of the military aid Congress approves for it effectively as a gift card to buy U.S.-made weapons."

Just listening to Harris during her CNN interview, you'd be clueless about the realities that the UN high commissioner for human rights, Volker Türk, spelled out in a statement midway through August: "The people of Gaza are now grieving 40,000 Palestinian lives lost, according to Gaza's health ministry. Most of the dead are women and children. This unimaginable situation is overwhelmingly due to recurring failures by the Israeli Defense Forces to comply with the rules of war. On average, about 130 people have been killed every day in Gaza over the past 10 months. The scale of the Israeli military's destruction of homes, hospitals, schools and places of worship is deeply shocking."

Notably, Harris gave no indication of the number of Palestinian lives lost – while she did say that 1,200 Israelis, including "many young people," lost their lives on October 7. That most of the Palestinians who died were children and women went unmentioned.

While the vice president said that Israelis were "massacred," she relied on passive voice to say only that too many Palestinians "have been killed."

After recording the interview, I transcribed it in full:

CNN'S Dana Bash: "President Biden has tried unsuccessfully to end the war between Israel and Hamas in Gaza. He's been doing it for months and months along with you. Would you do anything differently, for example would you withhold some U.S. weapons shipments to Israel? That's what a lot of people on the progressive left want you to do."

Harris: "Let me be very clear. I am unequivocal and unwavering in my commitment to Israel's defense and its ability to defend itself, and that's not gonna change. But let's take a step back. October 7. Twelve hundred people are massacred, many young people who are simply attending a music festival. Women were horribly raped. As I said then I say today, Israel had a right, has a right to defend itself. We would. And how it does so matters. Far too many innocent Palestinians have been killed, and we have got to get a deal done. We were in Doha, we have to get a deal done, this war must end –"

Bash: "And in the meantime –"

Harris: "And we must get a deal that is about getting the hostages out. I've met with the families of the American hostages. Let's get the hostages out. Let's get the ceasefire done."

Bash: "But no change in policy? In terms of arms and so forth."

Harris: "No. We have to get a deal done. Dana, we have to get a deal done. When you look at the significance of this to the families, to the people who are living in that region, a deal is not only the right thing to do to end this war, but will unlock so much of what must happen next. I remain committed, since I've been on October 8, to what we must do to work toward a two-state solution, where Israel is secure and in equal measure the Palestinians have security and self-determination and dignity."

When I heard Harris say "I remain committed," I felt sure that the phrase "two-state solution" could not be far behind. For U.S. politicians and pundits, it has become a handy slogan to assert virtuous intent – rendered more and more absurd as Israel's terroristic ethnic cleansing persists in Gaza and escalates in the occupied West Bank. And as genocide continues to gain momentum.

There is every reason to believe that Donald Trump – who said this summer that the president should let Israel "finish the job" – would be even worse than Biden as an accomplice to Israel's slaughter of Palestinian people. But that's no reason to evade the unconscionable complicity of President Biden in the daily mass atrocities.

A suction tube of euphemisms and evasion has captured many a partisan mind. And so it was from the podium of the Democratic National Convention, when the usually admirable Representative Alexandria Ocasio-Cortez descended into making the groundless claim that Harris "is working tirelessly to secure a ceasefire in Gaza and bringing the hostages home."

In sharp contrast, with horrors in Gaza continuing, fellow Democratic Representative Rashida Tlaib has never taken the easy way out. As she has done countless times since last fall, on Thursday she sent out a truthful and disturbing message.

"Palestinian Americans feel invisible, with our trauma and pain unseen and ignored by both Democrats and Republicans," Tlaib wrote. "We want action to stop the horrific massacres of our families and polling shows that, regardless of political party, the majority of Americans are with us.... Yet, even after over 600 weapons shipments since

October, including fighter jets, high explosive mortars, and more, the Biden administration has approved another $20 billion in weapons for the Israeli military to commit well-documented war crimes and continue to murder Palestinian children and civilians."

And Tlaib wrote: "An arms embargo to stop the genocide is not just the moral, just, and right thing to do. It is also good politics."

Whether Kamala Harris will ever really get the message is unclear.

Trump's Victory and Elite Power Over the Democratic Party

November 6, 2024

A PAIR OF QUOTES, SEPARATED BY EIGHT YEARS, SPOTLIGHT A chronic political mentality at the top of the Democratic Party:

"The path to victory in a state like Michigan, Harris campaign officials are betting, is through suburban counties that are home to many college-educated and white voters," the *New York Times* reported three weeks ago.

"For every blue-collar Democrat we lose in western Pennsylvania, we will pick up two moderate Republicans in the suburbs in Philadelphia. And you can repeat that in Ohio and Illinois and Wisconsin," Democratic Senator Chuck Schumer said in July 2016.

The same basic approach of Democratic Party elites that first opened the door to the White House for Donald Trump has done it again.

After losing a national election, political parties sometimes muster the wisdom to compile an "autopsy" report – assessing what went wrong and what changes are needed for the future. But after Hillary Clinton lost as a corporate war-hawk candidate in 2016, the Democratic National Committee showed that it had no interest in doing any such report.

So, at RootsAction we decided to do it ourselves, with a task force of researchers and activists who wrote *Autopsy: The Democratic Party in Crisis*. Many of our key findings about the 2016 election apply to the latest one. For example:

- "The Democratic National Committee and the party's congressional leadership remain bent on prioritizing the chase for elusive Republican voters over the Democratic base: especially people of color, young people and working-class voters overall."

- One of the large groups with a voter-turnout issue is young people, "who encounter a toxic combination of a depressed economic reality, GOP efforts at voter suppression, and anemic messaging on the part of Democrats."

- "Emerging sectors of the electorate are compelling the Democratic Party to come to terms with adamant grassroots rejection of economic injustice, institutionalized racism, gender inequality, environmental destruction and corporate domination. Siding with the people who constitute the base isn't truly possible when party leaders seem to be afraid of them."

- The Democratic Party's claims of fighting for "working families" have been undermined by its refusal to directly challenge corporate power, enabling Trump to masquerade as a champion of the people.

- "What must now take place includes honest self-reflection and confronting a hard truth: that many view the party as often in service to a rapacious oligarchy and increasingly out of touch with people in its own base." The Democratic Party should disentangle itself – ideologically and financially – from Wall Street, the military-industrial complex and other corporate interests that put profits ahead of public needs.

Four weeks ago, when asked on ABC's "The View" if she would have done anything differently than President Biden, the reply from Kamala Harris was more than notable: "Not a thing comes to mind."

Such loyalty to the powerful is a repetition compulsion disorder with horrendous consequences. Harris's reply – after a full year of ongoing mass murder and genocide in Gaza, made possible by U.S. military aid – was a moral failure and a prelude to electoral disaster. Harris stuck with her patron in the Oval Office and his role as an accomplice to Israel while disregarding the clear wishes of the Democratic Party's base.

Now that a fascistic party has won the presidency along with the Senate and apparently the House as well, the stakes for people and planet are truly beyond comprehension. Grassroots organizing should include maximum possible nonviolent pressure on officials in government and other institutions, insisting that compromise with Republican leaders is completely unacceptable.

"If you're not worried about encroaching fascism in America, before long it will start to feel normal. And when that happens, we're all in trouble," the author of *How Fascism Works*, Jason Stanley, warned in a video. That was six years ago.

"Normalization of fascist ideology, by definition, would make charges of 'fascism' seem like an overreaction, even in societies whose norms are transforming along these worrisome lines," Stanley wrote in his 2018 book. "Normalization means precisely that encroaching ideologically extreme conditions are not recognized as such because they have come to seem normal. The charge of fascism will always seem extreme; normalization means that the goalposts for the legitimate use of 'extreme' terminology continually move."

Resisting such normalization is now imperative.

Biden's Post-Election Pep Talk Was Pathetic – Democrats Must Prepare to Fight

November 8, 2024

AFTER YEARS OF SERVING AS ENABLERS FOR A FALTERING President Biden, Democrats in Congress must finally break away from his leadership – for the sake of their party and the survival of democracy in this country.

Donald Trump, the man whom General Mark Milley called "fascist to the core" and "the most dangerous person to this country," does not deserve to have the blue carpet rolled out for him at the White House. Yet such hospitality was key to Biden's message in his Rose Garden speech on Thursday.

It's one thing to pledge to "ensure a peaceful and orderly transition," as Biden did. It's quite another to proceed as though this is a normal transition and a normal incoming president.

Instead of rising to the historical moment with clarity about the grave and imminent challenges ahead, Biden opted for ominous silence about the clear and present danger to the republic that America will face beginning January 20, 2025.

To the tens of millions of Americans who are deeply alarmed about the future of this country under a second Trump administration, Biden offered only some of his usual aphorisms, along with vague pep-talk phrases like "setbacks are unavoidable, but giving up is unforgivable."

When Biden assured the nation that "we're going to be okay," the statement failed to live up to his responsibilities as someone who took an oath to "preserve, protect and defend the Constitution of the United States."

That Constitution is now under dire threat. But you wouldn't know it from what Biden had to say. Instead, what screamed out were his silences, as though the well-founded and widespread worries about Trump's fascistic qualities are no longer of great moment.

In effect, Biden began to blaze a post-election trail of conciliation toward the extremist politics of the present-day Republican Party. If congressional Democrats follow along that path, they will compound their grievous error of serving as yes-men and yes-women for Biden's insistence on running for re-election, until his disastrous debate performance.

A huge looming question now is whether Democrats in office will fold up their tents and retreat – or fight back against the Trump forces that are on the march.

It's long past time for Democrats on Capitol Hill to stop playing follow-the-leader and start providing actual leadership worthy of their constituents. For one thing, members of Congress should refuse to echo Biden's post-election rhetoric and instead speak plainly and forcefully about the rough road ahead to protect civil liberties and the rule of law.

In particular, Democrats in the Senate should make full use of the two months ahead. Those who can wield committee gavels before the changeover should hold high-profile hearings to spotlight vital facts about the Trump record, his threats to democracy and the enormous dangers that the Project 2025 agenda poses.

Looking ahead to next year, Democrats should jettison the standard rhetoric about reaching across the aisle. Voters who elected Democrats will not take kindly to odors of capitulation to the GOP. And in 2026, those who behave as quislings will risk vigorous primary challenges.

In a word, what the Democratic base has been yearning for – leadership – needs to emerge from the party's lawmakers who have been tragically willing to go along with the catastrophic political edicts from the Biden White House and the Democratic National Committee. What's past is prologue, but retrospective understanding could help light a fire under elected Democrats who wasted years publicly supporting the idea of Biden running for re-election while privately bemoaning it.

Biden has squandered the immediate post-election period by setting a bad example for Democrats. It's a pattern that has been integral to the chain of events that led to the very long delay in his departure from the 2024 race and a badly truncated campaign by Vice President Kamala Harris.

The futures of the Democratic Party and the nation as a constitutional republic are inextricably intertwined. To be sure, that's not because of any great virtue to be found within the Democratic Party. The reality is that in the two-party system, the Democrats are the only bulwark against the runaway power of the Trump-MAGA Republican Party – and the transformative agenda so clearly and ominously mapped out by Project 2025.

Right now, huge numbers of Americans are holding their breath, with great trepidation, to see if "the system" can withstand the massive stress test ahead. The Democratic Party has failed to avert this existential crisis for our nation as the vaunted land of the free. To avert irreversible catastrophe, the historic burden now falls on Democrats in elected positions to step up to their responsibilities at last.

Looming Fascism and the Question of Hope

November 13, 2024

WHEN SOME LEADING THINKERS AT THE LONDON SCHOOL OF Economics saw fascism take hold in the 1930s, Oxford history professor Ben Jackson said in a recent BBC interview, they "argued that in those circumstances the people with economic power in society, the property owners, are willing to cancel democracy, cancel civil liberties, and make deals with political organizations like the Nazis if it guarantees their economic interest."

That analysis has an ominous ring to it now as many tech industrialists swing behind President-elect Trump.

"Big congratulations to our 45th and now 47th President on an extraordinary political comeback and decisive victory," Amazon founder Jeff Bezos tweeted the morning after the election. Weeks earlier, as the owner of the *Washington Post*, Bezos had blocked an endorsement of Kamala Harris by the newspaper's editorial board.

Bezos could lose billions of dollars in antitrust cases, but now stands a better chance of winning thanks to a second Trump administration. During the last decade, Amazon Web Services gained huge contracts with the federal government, including a $10 billion deal with the National Security Agency.

No wonder Bezos' post-election tweet laid it on thick – "wishing @ realDonaldTrump all success in leading and uniting the America we all love."

Not to be left behind at the starting gun in the tech industry's suck-up-to-Trump derby, Meta's CEO Mark Zuckerberg wrote: "Congratulations to President Trump on a decisive victory. We have great opportunities ahead of us as a country. Looking forward to working with you and your administration."

As a nine-figure donor and leading purveyor of online lies for the 2024 Trump campaign, Elon Musk has been working closely with Trump. The Tesla magnate, X (formerly Twitter) owner and SpaceX mogul is well-positioned to help shape policies of the incoming administration. A week after the election, news broke that Musk has been chosen by Trump to co-lead an ill-defined "Department of Government Efficiency" with an evident mission to slash the public sector.

Musk, Bezos and Zuckerberg rank first, third and fourth respectively on the *Forbes* list of the world's richest individuals. The three of them have combined wealth of around $740 billion.

"In recent years, many tech elites have shrugged off the idealism once central to Silicon Valley's self-image, in favor of a more corporate and transactional approach to politics," the *Washington Post* gingerly reported after the election. The newspaper added: "A growing contingent of right-wing tech figures argue that Trump can usher in a new era of American dominance by removing red tape."

For amoral gazillionaires like Bezos and Musk, ingratiating themselves with Trump is a wise investment that's calculated to yield windfall returns. Evidently, the consequences in human terms are of no real concern. In fact, social injustice and the divisions it breeds create the conditions for still more lucrative political demagoguery, with the richest investors at the front of the line to benefit from corporate tax cuts and regressive changes in individual tax brackets.

After Election Day, the fascism scholar Jason Stanley offered a grim appraisal: "People who feel slighted (materially or socially) come to accept pathologies – racism, homophobia, misogyny, ethnic nationalism, and religious bigotry – which, under conditions of greater equality, they would reject. And it is precisely those material conditions for a healthy, stable democracy that the United States lacks today. If anything, America has come to be singularly defined by its massive wealth inequality, a phenomenon that cannot but undermine social cohesion and breed resentment."

The threat of fascism in the United States is no longer conjectural. It is swiftly gathering momentum, fueled by the extremism of the party set to soon control both the executive and legislative branches of the U.S. government as well as most of the federal court system.

It's not only that, as Stanley notes, "the Republican Party's domination of all branches of government would render the U.S. a one-party state." Already set in motion are cascading toxic effects on social discourse and political dynamics, marked by widening acceptance and promotion of overt bigotries and brandished hatreds.

The successful relaunch of Trump's political quest has again rocketed him into the stratosphere of power. Corporate profits for the few will reach new heights. Only humanity will suffer.

This deeply perilous time requires realism – but not fatalism. In the worst of times, solidarity is most needed.

And what about hope?

Consider what Fred Branfman had to say.

In the late 1960s, Fred was a humanitarian-aid volunteer in Laos when he discovered that his country was taking the lives of peasants there by the thousands. He assembled *Voices from the Plain of Jars*, a book with the subtitle "Life Under an Air War," published in 1972. It included essays by Laotian people living under long-term U.S. bombardment along with drawings by children who depicted the horrors all around them.

When I asked Fred to describe his experience in Laos, he said: "At the age of 27, a moral abyss suddenly opened before me. I was shocked to the core of my being as I found myself interviewing Laotian peasants, among the most decent, human and kind people on Earth, who described living underground for years on end, while they saw countless fellow villagers and family members burned alive by napalm, suffocated by 500-pound bombs, and shredded by antipersonnel bombs dropped by my country, the United States."

Fred moved to Washington, where he worked with antiwar groups to lobby Congress and protest the inflicting of mass carnage on Indochina. During the decades that followed, he kept working as a writer and activist to help change policies, stop wars, and counteract what he described as "the effect on the biosphere of the interaction between global warming, biodiversity loss, water aquifer depletion, chemical contamination, and a wide variety of other new threats to the biospheric systems upon which human life depends."

When I talked with Fred a few years before his death in 2014, he said: "I find it hard to have much 'hope' that the species will better itself in coming decades."

But, Fred went on, "I have also reached a point in my self-inquiries where I came to dislike the whole notion of 'hope.' If I need to have 'hope' to motivate me, what will I do when I see no rational reason for hope? If I can be 'hopeful,' then I can also be 'hopeless,' and I do not like feeling hopeless."

He added: "When I looked more deeply at my own life, I noticed that my life was not now and never had been built around 'hope.' Laos was an example. I went there, I learned to love the peasants, the bombing shocked my psyche and soul to the core, and I responded – not because I was hopeful or hopeless, but because I was alive."

We're alive. Let's make the most of it, no matter how much hope we have. What we need most of all is not optimism but determination.

2025 And Beyond

Two events in November showed the huge gap between the potential for true progressive change and the dire reality of Democratic Party leadership.

When socialist Zohran Mamdani won election as mayor of New York, he said: "If there is any way to terrify a despot, it is by dismantling the very conditions that allowed him to accumulate power. This is not only how we stop Trump; it's how we stop the next one."

A week later, eight members of the Senate's Democratic caucus surrendered to President Trump, betraying efforts to defend Obamacare and a health-care status quo that still left tens of millions uninsured or underinsured. The capitulation meant that the nation's health care would get even worse.

Unless Democrats really put up a fight against the pseudo-populism of the rapacious and fascistic Trump regime, they're unlikely to regain the support of the working-class voters who have deserted them.

An ominous future is calling for courage and solidarity.

FREE SPEECH WILL BE STRICTLY ENFORCED

All of the Future at Stake

DURING THE YEAR AFTER DONALD TRUMP WON THE presidency again, Democratic Party leaders were mostly in restrained disarray. Vast numbers of people who had expected Trump 2.0 to be disastrous were taken aback by just how terrible 2025 quickly became. But the behaviors of top-ranking Democrats in Congress and the Democratic National Committee fell far short of meeting the dire moment. They were hidebound, rarely creative and routinely conformist – refusing to respond in ways that measured up to coping with constant emergencies doing enormous damage. The combination of fascistic Republican power and uninspiring Democratic leadership foreshadowed even worse calamities.

As the top Democrats in government, Senator Chuck Schumer and Representative Hakeem Jeffries have been symptoms and perpetrators of the party's afflictions – unable to convincingly pose as fighters for the working class. Their strongest affinities have remained elsewhere. Aside from rhetorical flourishes at times, the pair doubled down on making nice with corporate America and wealthy donors while alternating between conciliation and rote partisanship toward the rival party.

The judicial system offered scant relief from the consolidation of autocratic power in the Oval Office. The Supreme Court rarely did anything about lawful lower-court rulings other than overturn them and side with Trump. With the top court steadily compliant, the executive and legislative branches were in the firm grip of people ignoring or destroying laws they didn't like.

So, as a practical matter, a crucial tool for salvaging elements of democracy in the United States would be electoral, while growing social movements would be vital. As when millions of protesters turned out during each No Kings Day in 2025, grassroots movement organizing could mobilize in big ways that the Democratic Party could not. Yet ousting Republicans from control of the federal government would necessarily involve electing enough candidates with a "D" after their names.

Lackluster Democratic Party leadership – coloring inside corporate lines while enmeshed with rich backers – hardly offers a plausible way to defeat the Trump forces, much less advance a humane political agenda. Saving the country from further descent into autocracy requires recognizing and overcoming the chokehold that Democratic leaders have on the party.

– – – –

Ambition and fear – striving to curry favor with the party hierarchy and being careful not to antagonize it – were central to the dynamics that enabled the disaster of the Biden re-election campaign to go forward until too late. Schumer served as a key enabler. His public megaphone and party authority mostly drowned out other Senate Democrats. "I talk to President Biden regularly, sometimes several times in a week, or usually several times in a week," Schumer said from a podium on Capitol Hill in mid-February 2024. "His mental acuity is great, it's fine, it's as good as it's been over the years…. He's fine. All this right-wing propaganda that his mental acuity has declined is wrong."

In 2025, Schumer's prominence was conspicuously harmful to the party's prospects. But – in a silent echo of their acquiescence to the ill-fated Biden '24 campaign – Schumer's Democratic colleagues stayed publicly mum about the ample reasons why Schumer should step aside from the spotlight role of their leader. A caricature of a wheeler-dealer pol in office too long, Schumer was a gift who kept on giving to Republicans as he reinforced the public image of Democrats as timeworn hacks while alienating and exasperating Democratic voters across the country.

Schumer became so unpopular with the Democratic base that he abruptly "postponed" – and didn't reschedule – a March 2025 speaking tour for his new book. An eruption of anger at his support for Trump's spending bill earlier in the month made Schumer realize that being confronted by irate Democrats in deep-blue states wouldn't make for good photo ops. Yet to Schumer, leaving his Senate leadership post was unthinkable. "Look, I'm not stepping down," he said in a TV network interview.

So, Schumer remained entrenched as central casting for the kind of leader that his party's usual voters clearly didn't want. Midway through 2025, a poll found that 62 percent of self-identified Democrats agreed "the leadership of the Democratic Party should be replaced with new people." And key findings from that Reuters/Ipsos survey meant that Schumer was the party's most important out-of-step leader.

A large majority of Democrats wanted elected officials to reduce "corporate influence," the poll showed, while a whopping 86 percent "said changing the federal tax code so wealthy Americans and large corporations pay more in taxes should be a priority." But Schumer's record is the epitome of corporate influence. For decades, he has given priority to protecting the financial interests of the wealthy and large corporations.

Schumer's unwelcome nickname – "the senator from Wall Street" – is longstanding and well-earned. He reached new heights as corporate America's champion on Capitol Hill during the severe financial crisis in 2008 – when he "became one of the first officials to promote a Wall Street bailout," the *New York Times* reported. The newspaper added that Schumer was playing "an unrivaled role in Washington as beneficiary, advocate and overseer of an industry that is his hometown's most important business."

Not surprisingly, by the time autumn 2009 arrived, more than 15 percent of the year's contributions from Wall Street to all senators had gone to Schumer.

Schumer has remained closely aligned with the very corporate interests that most Democratic voters don't want party leaders to serve. Meanwhile, floods of appreciative donations have poured into Schumer's campaign coffers from such sectors as the banking, real estate, financial and tobacco industries. At the end of 2024, Schumer's campaign committee reported a six-year donor haul of nearly $43 million. More than one-quarter of that total came just from securities and investment companies, real estate interests, law firms and lawyers.

By clinging to his Senate minority leader post, Schumer continued to damage the capacity of the Democratic Party to rebound from its grave 2024 setbacks and its ongoing abysmal approval ratings. More to the point, Democratic senators chose to passively keep him as their top leader.

– – – –

Meanwhile, as the country reeled from the Trump regime's systematic assault on human rights and the rule of law, Schumer's counterpart in the House of Representatives was doing his part to maintain the Democratic Party's fidelity to the old ways. Hakeem Jeffries, nearly 20 years younger than Schumer, had also risen through the ranks as a devotee of top-down politics animated by the lure of big checks.

The week after Trump's return to the Oval Office, Jeffries traveled to California and met with donor powerhouses in Silicon Valley, where he reportedly "said Democrats were reaching toward the center, while Trump will swing harder right." In effect, while aspiring to be the next House speaker, Jeffries was pledging not to stay too far away from Trump's ever more extreme right-wing politics.

Jeffries went on to laud former President Biden as a present-day political guide. In April 2025, when Biden delivered his first post-presidency speech, Jeffries told reporters: "This is an all hands on deck moment, which is why President Biden's voice in this moment is so important." Jeffries made the comment shortly after a CNN poll asked Democratic voters "which one person best reflects the core values of the Democratic Party" – and only 1 percent chose Biden.

While indicating that he was stuck in the past, the party's House leader also demonstrated that he was slow on the uptake. Midway through May, Jeffries sent out a fundraising text saying that he "recently announced a 10-point plan to take on Trump and the Republicans." But the plan was no more recent than early February, just two weeks after Trump's inauguration. It was hardly reassuring that the House minority leader cited a 100-day-old memo as his strategy for countering the administration's countless moves since then to dismantle entire government agencies, attack civil rights, undermine a wide range of civil liberties and destroy life-saving programs.

Claims that Jeffries and Schumer were champions of working people clashed with the duo's eagerness to please wealthy contributors by protecting their interests. And much like their estrangement from the progressive economic views of the party's base, Schumer and Jeffries were locked into automatic support for Israel despite the outlooks of voters they supposedly represented. In August 2025, the Economist/YouGov Poll asked Democrats this question: "Do you think that Israel is committing genocide against Palestinian civilians?" Here are the results: Yes, 65 percent. No, 8 percent. "Not sure," 27 percent.

At the same time, the Democratic Party could hardly afford to further alienate its base. In late summer, the *New York Times* published an in-depth analysis of voter registration data, with stunning conclusions: "The Democratic Party is hemorrhaging voters long before they even go to the polls. Of the 30 states that track voter registration by political party, Democrats lost ground to Republicans in every single one between the 2020 and 2024 elections – and often by a lot. That four-year swing toward the Republicans adds up to 4.5 million voters, a deep political hole that could take years for Democrats to climb out from."

The possibility that the Democratic Party could actually climb out of the "deep political hole" was especially remote because its leaders continued to function as if navigating politics in some bygone era.

– – – –

Schumer's devotion to the politics of big money and reflexive backing of Israel intersected with his refusal to endorse Zohran Mamdani, the 2025 Democratic candidate for mayor of New York. The Senate's leading Democrat, a lifelong New York City resident, could not bring himself to side with the party's nominee.

The insurgent candidate, propelled by tens of thousands of volunteers, had decisively beaten the disgraced former governor Andrew Cuomo in the Democratic primary. In the general election, Mamdani again faced Cuomo, who was running on a newly created ballot line. Endorsing Mamdani should have been a no-brainer for Schumer. But he could not abide what Mamdani stood for – full support for economic justice and human rights, including the rights of Palestinian people being subjected to ethnic cleansing, mass murder and genocide.

Some billionaires went ballistic against Mamdani. A social-media screed by hedge-fund manager Bill Ackman (net worth: upward of $9 billion) was damn near apoplectic that activists and voters had so terribly transgressed. Ackman described himself as "a supporter of President Trump" while expressing a fervent desire "to save the Democratic Party from itself." Mamdani's policies, Ackman wrote after his primary win, "would be disastrous for NYC. Socialism has no place in the economic capital of our country."

Another billionaire, Michael Bloomberg, had pumped $5 million into a super PAC behind Cuomo during the primary campaign. After Mamdani became the party's nominee, floodgates opened wider as ultra-wealthy magnates poured money into stop-Mamdani efforts. In late summer, 10 weeks before Election Day, *Truthout* reported:

As expected, billionaires and billionaire-owned companies such as Airbnb and DoorDash are now spending big to defeat Mamdani and influence the race.

An analysis of new campaign finance filings by influence trackers at the nonprofit public interest research organization LittleSis found that multiple billionaires and their companies have funneled more than $19 million into political action committees (PACs) that support Cuomo or oppose Mamdani and other candidates. With names such as Fix the City, Inc. and Affordable New York, such super PACS provide a vehicle for elite New Yorkers and corporate interests to influence public opinion on the race.

For example, the short-term rental company Airbnb reported a $5 million donation to Affordable New York, a group that has spent heavily on city races and reported spending $1.3 million opposing Mamdani and his progressive ally, city comptroller Brad Lander. According to SEC filings, Airbnb's three billionaire co-founders – Brian Chesky, Nathan Blecharczyk, and Joe Gebbia – collectively control 79 percent of the voting power at the company.

By refusing to endorse Mamdani, while participating in sly nods to completely false charges of antisemitism, Schumer was in tacit league with the billionaires furiously trying to prevent a popular democratic socialist from becoming mayor. For his part, Jeffries waited four months after the primary until endorsing Mamdani just before voting began in the general election "Worst of all, Democrats like Schumer and Jeffries are shooting their party in the foot," *The New Republic* senior editor Alex Shephard wrote in September. "Mamdani is a dynamic, charismatic candidate unlike any the party has seen for years. In June, he beat Cuomo, a former governor, by more than 10 points by activating middle-class voters... Predominantly renters, Mamdani's voters were also disproportionately young, Asian, and Hispanic – all groups that moved toward Trump in last year's election, and that Democrats will need if they want to take back Congress and the White House."

– – – –

The sordid tale of the party establishment's response to the Mamdani campaign ran parallel to the saga of two Gaza resolutions at the semi-annual meeting of the Democratic National Committee in late August 2025. It was the first DNC gathering convened by its new chair

Ken Martin; he had replaced Jaime Harrison, whose four-year term was marked by steady subservience to his patron Joe Biden.

The new meeting gave the governing body of the Democratic Party a chance to finally oppose the U.S. government's arming of the Israeli government while it engaged in genocide. But the DNC's leadership was determined to derail a resolution calling for "an arms embargo and suspension of military aid to Israel."

Maneuvering to sidetrack that resolution, Martin and all five vice chairs sponsored a counter-resolution doing little more than repeat the kind of hollow rhetoric that President Biden and Vice President Harris had offered as the Gaza massacres continued during their last 15 months in office. Martin and the vice chairs "aimed to blunt the power of the resolution on Gaza by introducing their own, watered-down resolution that stops far short of calling for an end to arms shipments to Israel," my RootsAction colleague Sam Rosenthal pointed out.

The tactic was reminiscent of the approach that had helped to defeat the Democratic ticket the previous year, when pre-election polling clearly showed that opposition to arming Israel was a majority view among voters. Recycling much the same approach in summer 2025 was even more oblivious to the roar of public opinion.

On the eve of the DNC meeting, I put a question to the most powerful vice chair, Jane Kleeb (also the president of the ASDC association of state party chairs, "the only national party organization focused exclusively on the current and future needs of State Democratic Parties"). Did she support or oppose, or have a neutral position on, the arms-embargo resolution? Kleeb would only reply: "I've sponsored a resolution on Gaza with other officers. I hope everyone comes to the table with agreed upon joint language."

The DNC member sponsoring the arms-embargo resolution, Allison Minnerly, was a 26-year-old youth organizer in Central Florida. Minnerly told me that she wasn't closed to the possibility of accepting amendments to her resolution, but it must "keep the core message." That message – "an arms embargo and suspension of military aid to Israel" – was exactly what provoked such strong opposition from DNC leaders. Their counter-resolution didn't even slightly criticize Israel for its large-scale killing of Palestinian people, by then in its twenty-third month.

Just days earlier, the *Guardian* had reported that "figures from a classified Israeli military intelligence database indicate five out of six Palestinians killed by Israeli forces in Gaza have been civilians, an extreme rate of slaughter rarely matched in recent decades of warfare." The official estimate of the carnage in Gaza – 60,000 direct deaths, including 18,500 children – was very likely a significant undercount. Meanwhile, by providing upward of 69 percent of Israel's arms imports, the United States was making it all possible.

Along with backing from all the vice chairs, Martin's resolution got some outside help in the drafting process. "This resolution was crafted with the input of Democratic Majority for Israel, a group whose super PAC worked to oust former Representatives Jamaal Bowman and Cori Bush," *The Nation* reported. Predictably, Democratic Majority for Israel put out a press release denouncing the arms-embargo resolution. But by then, the accurate name for the group would be Democratic Minority for Israel.

One poll after another in 2025 found that – in the words of a summer headline over a Brookings Institution analysis – "support for Israel continues to deteriorate, especially among Democrats and young people." A Gallup poll in July found that only 8 percent of Democrats said they approved of Israel's military action in Gaza. The polling lined up with the conclusions from Human Rights Watch, Amnesty International and other (including Israeli) human rights organizations that unequivocally reported Israel was committing genocide in Gaza.

Minnerly's resolution for suspending military aid gained notable support from young Democratic leaders. The president of the official College Democrats of America organization (also a DNC member), Sunjay Muralitharan, tweeted: "As the National President of @ CollegeDems I'm proud to co-sponsor the DNC Resolution calling for an arms embargo and explicit recognition of a Palestinian State. Young Americans have made their voices clear. A modern Democratic Party must stand against global injustice." The chair of High School Democrats of America put out a similar statement.

But the DNC leadership stood its pro-Israel ground against a large majority of Democrats nationwide.

The top of the DNC power structure exerted pressure on Minnerly to dilute or withdraw her resolution, but she refused to be intimidated. When we spoke days before the meeting, her tone was measured, emphatic and resolute. In response to questions about her approach to organizing, she emphasized that "we don't wait for change: we create it. It isn't easy, but it's worth fighting for policies and ideals that represent you."

Abiding by the wishes of Chair Martin, the Resolutions Committee unanimously approved his counter-resolution and then – with an unaccountable voice vote – overwhelmingly defeated Minnerly's resolution. Martin then withdrew his counter-resolution and announced he would appoint a "task force" to study issues related to Israel and Palestinians. While civilians in Gaza continued to die from bombs, bullets and starvation, the DNC was in no rush to question the status quo.

The Democratic National Committee's leadership was simultaneously guilty of political malpractice and moral depravity – actively complicit with what most of the nation's Democrats understood to be genocide. The DNC thus continued its drift into a sealed-off political galaxy, far away from where most Democrats actually were in the United States.

The party's distance from young adults was especially huge. And power-broker Democrats persisted in the political equivalent of eating – or even discarding – the party's seed corn, with little regard for much of a future. Inevitably, every election cycle, more young voters would be replacing old ones. But party leaders did not seem to grasp or care that moral politics and pragmatic politics could boost each other – or that spurning moral politics could be the opposite of pragmatic.

– – – –

"It should come as no great surprise that a Democratic Party which has abandoned working class people would find that the working class has abandoned them," Senator Bernie Sanders tweeted immediately after the 2024 election. "While the Democratic leadership defends the status quo, the American people are angry and want change."

A year later, the Democratic Party seemed mostly stuck in the mud of the past, as if mired in the Joe Biden era of pinning election hopes on revulsion toward Donald Trump. Yes, the cascading horrors of Trump 2.0 called for fierce opposition – but just denouncing the regime's bottomless pit of evils was not a good bet for ending GOP control of Congress in 2026 or the presidency in 2028.

President Biden's unspeakably tragic refusal to forgo running for re-election until far too late was enabled by top-to-bottom party dynamics and a follow-the-leader conformity that remains all too real. Pandering to potential big donors – part and parcel of what Sanders described as abandoning the working class – can easily seem like just another day in elected office.

A story about California Governor Gavin Newsom, often touted as perhaps the leading Democratic contender for president in 2028, is in the category of "you can't make this stuff up." As *Politico* reported in the spring of 2025, he was "making sure California's business elite can call him, maybe. Roughly 100 leaders of state-headquartered companies have received a curious package in recent months: a prepaid, inexpensive cell phone... programmed with Newsom's digits and accompanied by notes from the governor himself. 'If you ever need anything, I'm a phone call away,' read one note to a prominent tech firm CEO, printed on an official letterhead, along with a hand-scrawled addendum urging the executive to reach out... It was Newsom's idea, a representative said, and has already yielded some 'valuable interactions.'"

There were, of course, no reports of Newsom sending cell phones programmed with his number to advocates for the working class and social justice. If they awaited a message from Newsom like "If you ever need anything, I'm a phone call away," the wait would most likely last forever.

Newsom could be understood as a cautionary case of a presidential hopeful giving opportunism a bad name as he moved rightward. During years as California's governor, he got into a rhythm of vetoing state legislation that would have helped domestic workers, farm workers, undocumented immigrants and striking workers.

In the age of Elon Musk, Jeff Bezos, Mark Zuckerberg and the like – with iron heels of mega-capital marching along while crushing democratic structures – Newsom has been among the Democratic elites racing to stay within shouting distance of oligarchs and their allies. At the same time, in some arenas, Newsom has pushed back against Trump.

As the decade entered its second half, progressives faced the paradoxical challenge of helping to build a united front inclusive of anti-Trump corporatists and militarists, even while fighting against corporatism and militarism. The need involved a dialectical approach, recognizing the twin imperatives of defeating a viciously anti-democratic Republican Party while working to gain enough power to implement truly humane agendas.

For those agendas, electoral campaigns and their candidates are vital – and should be energized as subsets of social movements, not the other way around.

If a fascistic takeover of the federal government continues, any possibility of fulfilling a progressive agenda would go out the Overton window along with residual elements of democracy. Words of the young Black Panther Party leader Fred Hampton, murdered in 1969 by the Chicago police (colluding with the FBI), ring profoundly true now: "Nothing is more important than stopping fascism, because fascism will stop us all."

What has routinely passed for the Democratic Party's opposition to the Trump regime comes across as little more than forgettable rhetoric and rote activities. Holding town halls around the country, or raising money to file lawsuits against the Trump administration's lawless actions, or appealing for funds to defeat Republicans in the next election are all well and good. But simply following party "leadership" that isn't leading much of anywhere is no substitute for daily grassroots outreach and systematic organizing in communities nationwide.

"An individual is no match for history," says the narrator of a novel by the Chilean anti-fascist Roberto Bolaño. That observation might not be open to dispute. But many individuals propelling social movements can be another matter.

Ω